JULIAN HAWTHORNE

Incredible Mysteries: Unsolved Disappearances Vol. 3

Contents

Louis Mackerley — 1

Ana Walshe — 7

Dee Ann Warner — 17

Jason Jolkowski — 24

Kelli Cribbs Abad — 30

Ebby Steppach — 36

Angela Whalen Hudson — 47

Audrey Moran & Jonathan Reynoso — 53

Heather Teague — 62

Michael McClain — 70

Laureen Rahn — 74

Nefertiri Trader — 86

Asha Kreimer — 92

Jake Latiolais — 97

Maureen Fields — 104

Daniel Robinson — 122

Luke Joly-Durocher — 133

Gwendolyn Brunelle — 139

Echo Lloyd — 145

Paul Stevenson — 153

Louis Mackerley

L ouis Anthony Mackerley, a bright-eyed boy with an infectious smile, was born into the loving arms of Harold and Sheila Mackerley on a cold winter's day, February 15, 1977, in the quaint town of Stanhope, New Jersey. The Mackerley household was a bustling hive of activity, with Louis being the cherished younger brother in a lively family. He looked up to his elder brother Harold, a nine-year-old with a protective streak, and cherished his role as the doting big brother to three-year-old Sheila and baby Edward, who was just five months old at the time.

In June of 1983, the Mackerleys, seeking new opportunities and adventures, uprooted their lives and moved to the historic city of Allentown, Pennsylvania. This move brought new friends, new experiences, and a new school for Louis, who was now a bright-eyed first-grader at Central Elementary.

Fast forward to June 7, 1984, a day etched in the memories of the Mackerley family. On this seemingly ordinary afternoon, seven-year-old Louis, full of energy and excitement, bounded home from school. He had plans, plans to meet friends just two blocks away in the 300 block of Chu Street. He asked his older brother, Harold, to join him, but Harold, engrossed in his favorite TV show, declined. Unfazed, Louis set out alone, his heart set on an afternoon of play and laughter with his friends. However, fate had other plans, and Louis never made it to his destination.

Back at home, Louis's aunt, who was babysitting that day, expected him to return by his usual time of 9:30 p.m., as it was not uncommon for him to stay out playing until then. But as the clock ticked past the hour and the night grew darker, a sense of unease began to settle over the Mackerley household.

Sheila Mackerley, Louis's mother, was in the hospital recovering from surgery when she was hit by a wave of maternal instinct – something was amiss. Her concern grew into alarm when Louis failed to return for dinner, an unusual occurrence for the otherwise punctual boy.

The family, now deeply worried, began a frantic search through the streets of Allentown. Sheila, still weak from her surgery, joined in, her mother's heart refusing to rest. But as hours passed with no sign of Louis, the sinking realization that he was truly missing gripped them.

At 11:10 p.m., with heavy hearts, the Mackerleys reported their son missing. What followed was an extensive and desperate search for the young boy, involving the community and authorities, but Louis seemed to have vanished without a trace.

Witness accounts began to surface. People recalled seeing Louis that afternoon, his path weaving between 4th Street and Garden Street, near the family's second-floor apartment. The most intriguing lead came from Marco, the owner of Marco's Doggy Shop. Louis had entered his shop around 4 p.m., lingering for about 45 minutes. He confided in Marco that he was hiding from two teenage boys. After leaving the shop around 4:45 p.m., Louis was seen heading towards Gordon Street.

The police questioned the two teenagers Louis had mentioned, but they were quickly ruled out in connection with his disappearance. The Mackerleys believed that after leaving the hot dog store, Louis might have been heading to 391 Chu Street, the home of an elderly woman named Helen, beloved by the neighborhood children, including Louis. Sadly, he never arrived there, and his whereabouts remain a mystery to this day.

In a twist that added layers of complexity to the already baffling case a new witness emerged, offering a potentially significant piece of information. This individual reported seeing the seven-year-old engaging in conversation with an unidentified man and woman near Jordan Creek, a location ominously close to his family home. The timing of this sighting, around 4:30 pm on the day Louis vanished, and its proximity to the Mackerley residence, cast a new shadow of suspicion over the events of that day.

This sighting gained importance against the backdrop of a disturbing event from earlier in the year. In January 1984, a mere five months before he went missing, Louis shared a harrowing experience with his parents, a nurse, and a psychiatrist. He revealed that he had been molested by a couple he referred to as Frank and Elizabeth. Louis detailed how this couple had assaulted him on the railroad tracks near Jordan Street, an area perilously close to the Lehigh River. Furthermore, he recounted another terrifying incident where he was taken to an apartment in Allentown by the same couple and subjected to further abuse. The couple, he said, had threatened him with harm if he spoke of these incidents.

These revelations left the police deeply concerned for Louis's safety, fearing that he might have been a victim of abduction. The lack of last names or an address for the couple made further investigation challenging. While there were doubts about the existence of Frank and Elizabeth, given reports of Louis's vivid imagination, the seriousness of his allegations could not be ignored. When a child speaks of such grave matters, it is imperative to explore every possibility.

As the case unfolded, various individuals came under scrutiny. In 1988, a self-proclaimed private investigator from New York named David Riggs found himself entangled in the investigation. Arrested in Virginia for inappropriate and aggressive behavior towards children, Riggs pleaded guilty and was sentenced to a year in prison. The police delved into the possibility of Riggs's involvement in Louis's disappearance. However, they found no evidence linking him to the case, leading them to conclude that he was not a suspect.

Engulfed by the anguish of their son's disappearance, found themselves unable to remain in their home. Eleven months after Louis went missing, they moved from the place filled with memories of their lost son. They settled in the home of the elderly woman Helen, a figure of warmth and affection in Louis's life, who was relocating to a retirement home.

The Mackerley family, in the aftermath of their son Louis's disappearance, sought solace in familiarity and nostalgia. They harbored a hope, a faint glimmer that maybe, just maybe, Louis would return to a place he loved and often dreamt of living in one day. This longing led them to move into the house once owned by Helen, an elderly woman dear to Louis. It was a place filled with memories, a place where Louis had felt happy and safe. However, the cruel hand of fate dealt them another blow. As time passed, the financial strain became unbearable, and the family, unable to keep up with the mortgage payments, faced bankruptcy. With heavy hearts, they relocated to Effort, Pennsylvania, leaving behind the house on Chu Street, which now stands vacant, a silent witness to a family's unending grief.

Louis Mackerley was only seven years old when he vanished in 1984. His physical description was widely circulated: a Caucasian male, about four feet tall, weighing around 44 pounds, with dark blonde to brown hair and blue eyes. He was last seen wearing a distinctive outfit: a maroon, blue, green, and white striped short-sleeved shirt, blue trousers with a unique red 'doggie' tag on the back pocket, an elastic belt with a train-shaped buckle, pink socks, and brown shoes. Louis had several distinguishing marks, including two circular burn marks on the right side of his chest, and he had a characteristic slow gait, often leading with his head tilted downwards. Known for standing with his hands on his hips while talking, Louis was also recognizable by the absence of four front teeth at the time of his disappearance.

Despite facing learning and emotional challenges, including a diagnosis of hyperactivity that required Ritalin medication twice daily, Louis was described as a friendly and talkative boy. He was shy and often preferred solitude, and had a fear of sleeping alone. His educational struggles were evident in his short attention span and difficulty in writing, but these challenges did not diminish his warm and engaging personality.

After his disappearance, Louis's parents, Harold and Sheila, were engulfed in a nightmare. They were quickly cleared of any involvement, both having solid alibis - Harold at work and Sheila in the hospital. They opened their home to investigators and the media, demonstrating their willingness to do anything that might lead to finding their son. They cooperated fully with the police, even passing polygraph tests. Despite their cooperation, they couldn't escape the shadow of suspicion that occasionally fell upon them, adding to their immense suffering.

Over the years, numerous tips, leads, and sightings poured in from across the United States. Louis's face became a familiar sight on billboards and milk cartons, a silent plea for anyone who might recognize him to come forward. One particularly notable tip came from Budd Lake, New Jersey, leading to one of Louis's cousins, but Louis himself remained missing.

Abduction was considered the most likely scenario. Louis, known for his trust in adults, might have easily conversed with strangers, unaware of the potential dangers. The haunting question remained: did he encounter Frank and Elizabeth, the couple he had previously spoken about, after leaving the hot dog stand? If Louis's account of their threats was true, it was a chilling possibility that they might have followed through on their sinister warning. Yet, without concrete evidence, the truth behind Louis Mackerley's disappearance remains shrouded in mystery.

The Mackerleys continue to hold onto hope, believing that somewhere, somehow, their son is still out there, alive. The passage of time has done little to diminish their resolve, their love for Louis driving them to never give up the search for their missing boy.

Ana Walshe

Ana, a spirited and ambitious woman hailing from Serbia, embarked on a journey that would intricately weave her personal and professional life into a captivating tapestry. It was back in 2008, within the welcoming walls of the Wheatley Hotel in Lennox, that destiny played its hand. Ana, then the reservation manager, encountered Brian Walshe, a man who would later become a pivotal figure in her life's narrative.

At that time, Ana was navigating the complexities of her first marriage with Mark Nip. However, like the changing seasons, their union gradually drifted towards its conclusion, culminating in a divorce in 2014. This marked a new chapter for Ana, one where she would blend her passion for hospitality with an academic foundation in French language and literature from Belgrade University.

Her thirst for knowledge and professional growth led her to Cornell, where she earned a master certificate in Hospitality Management. This was just the beginning of a series of impressive director-level roles in major hospitality firms. By early 2022, Ana had ascended to the role of Operations Director at Tishman Spire in Washington DC, a testament to her relentless drive and expertise.

Parallel to her soaring career, Ana's heart found its true north. She and Brian Walshe united their lives in matrimony in 2015, embarking on a journey filled with love, laughter, and the bustling energy of three young boys, aged two to six. As the main breadwinner, Ana embodied the essence of a modern, empowered woman, balancing the demands of a thriving career with the joys and challenges of motherhood.

Brian, an Ivy League alumnus with a diverse educational background from prestigious institutions like Carnegie Mellon, the University of Massachusetts in Amherst, Northeastern University, and the JFK School of Government at Harvard, had his own share of ups and downs. Despite his privileged educational background, Brian faced a stumbling block in 2021 when he was entangled in legal issues, leading to a guilty plea on fraud charges related to selling counterfeit artwork.

This turn of events saw Brian under home confinement, his world shrinking to the confines of their family home, with only brief sojourns for essential errands. Meanwhile, Ana's world was ever-expanding. She juggled her time between the family's Massachusetts residence and a new home in DC, becoming a familiar face on flights between Boston's Logan Airport and Ronald Reagan National Airport.

But what truly set Ana apart was her radiant personality, a trait that endeared her to friends and colleagues alike. "She's just so personable; she lights up a room," they would say. "Ana's passion, fun, and joy are infectious. She's someone you're drawn to immediately, genuinely interested in everyone and everything – a beautiful, wonderful, passionate, joyful spirit."

It was this same spirit that illuminated the Walshe household on New Year's Eve, as they welcomed a close friend, Jim Mootloo, to celebrate with them. The evening was a cascade of laughter, toasts, and a lavish meal prepared by the couple, encapsulating the joy and hope that New Year's brings.

The dawn of New Year's Day unfolded with an unexpected turn in Brian and Ana's life. According to Brian, it was a morning like many they had shared, yet distinct in its sudden departure from routine. Ana, with her usual efficiency, got ready for the day. She shared a tender goodbye with Brian, urging him to catch a few more moments of sleep. Her mornings typically began early, usually between 6 and 7 AM, with a ride to the airport via Uber, Lyft, or taxi.

Ana had a flight booked to Washington D.C. for January 3rd, a return to her bustling work life after the holiday respite. However, that particular morning, she woke Brian with news of a work emergency, necessitating her departure earlier than planned. But, as the day unfolded, it became clear that something was amiss. Ana never showed up at the airport, and she didn't board her scheduled flight on January 3rd either.

By January 4th, concern was mounting. It was her Washington-based employer who first rang the alarm, contacting the Massachusetts police to report Ana missing. Brian, too, reported her disappearance around the same time. The unsettling truth was that no one had heard from Ana since the early hours of January 1st.

In his growing worry, Brian reached out to Ana's circle of friends. His calls were tinged with a hope for some reassuring news. "Good afternoon, it's Brian Walshe. I hope all is well. I'm just reaching out to everyone I can. Ana hasn't been in touch for a few days. Do you know anyone that might have had contact with her? Sorry to bother you, I'm sure everything's fine," he would say, trying to mask his growing concern.

The situation escalated on January 5th, when the Cohasset Police Department turned to the public for help. They sought any information or sightings of the 39-year-old mother. The press conference was a somber affair, with police from Cohasset, along with detectives from Massachusetts State Police and neighboring towns, appealing for leads. The police maintained that it was a missing person investigation, with no evidence at that point to suggest anything suspicious or criminal.

The case took a perplexing turn when it was revealed that there was no evidence that Ana had taken a ride-share to Logan Airport. Uber, Lyft, and local taxi companies had no record of a pickup at her address. Even a check of the home's ring camera system showed no sign of Ana leaving.

As January 6th and 7th came, the search efforts intensified. Law enforcement, aided by 20 troopers from a specialized search and rescue team, three police K-9 units, and a police helicopter, combed the woods about a mile from Ana's home. They scoured every inch, searching for any trace of what might have happened to Ana.

The search took on an increasingly desperate tone as State Police divers were called in to search a small stream and even drain the home's swimming pool. Despite these extensive efforts, after two full days, the state police announced their decision not to return for a third day. The woodland search, though exhaustive, had yielded no leads, deepening the mystery of Ana's disappearance.

On that fateful day, January 1st, Brian Walshe recounted a day that seemed ordinary on the surface. The babysitter arrived in the afternoon, and Brian left to run errands, including a trip to his mother's place in Swampscott, about an hour's drive away. However, a curious detail emerged: Brian had left without his cellphone, claiming it was lost the night before. This lack of GPS led to him getting lost, prolonging his absence that afternoon.

Brian's account of his day continued with a brief stop at his mother's, followed by errands at Whole Foods and CVS. But his journey was marked by further delays as he claimed to have gotten lost again, eventually returning home around 8 PM.

However, the veracity of Brian's detailed account began to unravel under scrutiny. Investigators spent days retracing his steps to Swampscott and meticulously reviewing hours of surveillance footage from Whole Foods and CVS. The outcome was startling – there was no trace of Brian Walshe at either location on the cameras. His confidently narrated itinerary for the day his wife went missing was, in fact, a fabrication.

Armed with this damning evidence, the Cohasset police arrested Brian for misleading a criminal investigation. His detailed but false statements had not only wasted precious time but also diverted the focus of the investigation.

On the eighth day after Ana's disappearance, the family's home in Cohasset became the center of a significant search operation. With Brian's consent, officers scoured the property and removed items, including a Volvo SUV. The house search, unlike the woodland one, revealed critical clues. In the basement, bloodstains and a damaged, bloody knife were discovered, a grim indicator of potential violence.

As the investigation deepened, attention turned to the data from Brian's cell phone, which, contrary to his earlier claims, had not been completely lost. He later revealed that one of his children had taken it during the New Year's Eve party and hidden it. Recovered data from the phone contradicted Brian's initial account, showing his travels to multiple undisclosed locations, which were also violations of his probation terms.

Meanwhile, data from Ana's cell phone painted a different picture from the narrative Brian had constructed. Her phone pinged in the area of their Cohasset home on January 1st, the day she was supposedly to have left, and intriguingly, again the next day.

In 2011, Brian Walshe found himself in South Korea, a country he had initially visited to attend a friend's wedding. The allure of the unfamiliar and the ties of an old friendship from his Carnegie Mellon undergraduate days convinced him to extend his stay. It was here, amidst the vibrant culture and bustling streets of South Korea, that Brian spotted an opportunity that would soon spiral into a complex web of deceit and art fraud.

Brian's friend, whom he was staying with, belonged to a family with a notable art collection, including pieces they were looking to sell. With his polished demeanor, education, and the air of generational wealth he exuded, Brian seemed like the perfect candidate to assist in this endeavor. His friend, placing trust in their shared history and Brian's apparent expertise, handed over a few precious pieces. Among them were a small Chinese statuette, a Keith Herring sketch, and two highly valued Andy Warhol paintings. These Warhols were part of the artist's famed 'Shadows' series, created in 1978-79, and the 'Dollar Sign' series, through which Warhol famously quipped, "Big Time art is Big Time money." Brian, embodying this sentiment, saw not just art but an opportunity.

Once in possession of these artworks, Brian's intentions veered drastically from helping his friend. His diary from the time reveals his real plan – to sell the art and pocket the proceeds for himself. "I have a plan for the art; need to get off with some of the good pieces. Hope I can make it through this one. It's going to be bumpy," he wrote, a foreshadowing of the convoluted path he was about to tread.

Over the next five years, Brian skillfully maneuvered through the international art market, selling the Warhol paintings multiple times to buyers worldwide. His first move was consigning both Warhols to Christie's Auction House in New York, where he managed to sell the 'Dollar Sign' for about $40,000. Not stopping there, he later employed a forger to create copies of these paintings, under the guise of needing them for insurance purposes. These forgeries were then sold as originals.

The FBI's investigation into these sales unveiled a trail of deception that spanned continents. For instance, in September 2015, Brian contracted to sell the 'Shadows' to an art consultant in Paris for $145,000. By the next year, he was found to have commissioned additional forgeries of the same series, this time without providing the originals – likely because he had already sold them. These forgeries even found their way onto eBay, where Brian, posing as a private collector, listed them for $100,000.

Ron Rivlin, a renowned art dealer specializing in Warhol, fell into Brian's trap, purchasing the 'Shadows' for $80,000. The deal seemed legitimate, complete with convincing documentation of authenticity, cleverly fabricated by Brian using paperwork from other buyers and galleries like Christie's in New York. However, the illusion shattered when Ron, an experienced collector with over a thousand Warhol artworks to his name, inspected the paintings and immediately noticed the fresh paint and unaged canvas. After a tense pursuit, Ron managed to recoup $30,000 of his investment, but by then, Brian had become elusive.

Ana, Brian's wife, was initially incredulous at the accusations against her husband. Her intervention led to Brian contacting Ron to work out a resolution, a move that revealed her own apprehension and fear amidst the unfolding scandal.

The FBI traced the proceeds of Brian's cons to his credit card, revealing exorbitant debts accrued from lavish travel and restaurant expenses. Severing ties with his friend in South Korea, Brian left the original artworks unreturned, his actions driven by a relentless pursuit of luxury and wealth. This was evident when, after securing $145,000 in Paris, he and Ana indulged in a shopping spree at Prada.

The art dealer who eventually uncovered Brian's complex web of deceit after five years highlighted the skills and aspects of his background that made him such a successful manipulator: his strong communication skills, likability, and the facade of wealth, including a multi-million-dollar home.

Brian Walshe's life story seems to eerily echo another of Andy Warhol's famous quotes: "Art is what you can get away with." His ventures into the world of art fraud, as concluded by the FBI, involved repeatedly selling counterfeit versions of Warhol's 'Shadows' paintings and, on at least two occasions, the 'Dollar Sign' series. But Brian's deceitful practices extended far beyond the art world.

Former friends of Brian revealed to the FBI a pattern of betrayal and theft. One college friend recounted how Brian had borrowed half a million dollars and never repaid it. Another friend detailed how Brian would regularly partake in lavish, expensive dinners, only to leave his friends with the bill. These actions were just the tip of the iceberg in a life marked by deception and manipulation.

The depth of Brian's estrangement from ethical behavior was further exposed following the death of his father, Dr. Thomas Walshe, in 2018. The elder Walshe, having been estranged from his son for nearly a decade, left Brian nothing but his "best wishes" in his will. This estrangement was rooted in a painful history: Brian had reportedly absconded with almost $1 million from his father, a theft so significant that it forced Dr. Walshe to continue working well past his desired retirement age.

Undeterred by the moral implications, Brian contested his father's will in court, ironically claiming it had been forged. Court documents from this legal battle painted a portrait of Brian as not just deceitful but also angry and violent. His past included treatment at the Austin Riggs Psychiatric Center in Stockbridge, Massachusetts, with a family friend claiming he had been diagnosed as a sociopath.

Despite these alarming revelations, those who knew Brian described him as lacking any overtly mean or aggressive demeanor. "He never even gave an angry stare," one acquaintance recalled. This lack of outward aggression perhaps made it easier for Brian to deceive those around him.

In 2021, Brian's pattern of fraudulent behavior led to a guilty plea on three federal fraud charges, resulting in house arrest and monitoring as he awaited sentencing. By January 2023, he was on probation but confined to his home, with strict restrictions on his movements. However, on January 2nd, a day when he should have been at home, Brian was captured on video at a Home Depot in Rockland, purchasing $450 worth of cleaning supplies, including mops, buckets, tarps, and various tapes – all paid for in cash and outside of his approved leave time.

The investigation into Ana's disappearance led police to search dumpsters near Brian's mother's home in Swampscott and a garbage collection transfer facility in Peabody. The findings from these searches were grim and disheartening, especially for those holding out hope for Ana. At the Swampscott site, police found bloody towels and other items matching those Brian purchased at Home Depot. The Peabody site yielded even more chilling evidence: a hacksaw, torn cloth, blood-stained materials, a hatchet, a rug, cleaning supplies, and trash bags. Law enforcement planned to test these blood samples against Walshe family members.

Already detained for misleading the investigation into his wife Ana's disappearance, Brian was then charged with her murder. Norfolk District Attorney Michael Morrissey publicly announced the charges, citing the development of probable cause based on Brian's misleading statements to investigators.

The pre-trial hearing for the murder charges laid bare the chilling details of the case, particularly the data retrieved from Brian's elusive cell phone and, astonishingly, his son's iPad. Brian's search history painted a macabre picture of a man meticulously planning to dispose of a body. His searches were disturbingly specific and graphic, including queries like how to dispose of a 115-pound woman's body, ways to stop a body from decomposing, and methods for cleaning blood from a wooden floor. These searches, timestamped in the early hours of January 1st, provided a haunting timeline of his intentions.

Further evidence showed Brian's presence at a Home Goods store in Norwell on January 2nd, where he purchased three rugs. Additional Google searches from that day included inquiries about dismembering a body and the possibility of being charged with murder without a body.

Amidst these chilling searches, a possible motive emerged. On December 27, 2022, Brian had searched for the best states to get a divorce. This, coupled with Ana's increasingly visible absence of her wedding ring on social media and her request for her mother to visit from Serbia, suggested turmoil in the Walshe marriage. Ana's high-powered job at an exclusive real estate agency contrasted sharply with Brian's role at home, hinting at potential tensions.

Financial motives also surfaced. Brian had searched online for the time required to wait for an inheritance. Since 2018, Ana had sold properties worth over $2.7 million and held a real estate portfolio estimated at $1.8 million, including properties in Lynn, Massachusetts, Baltimore, and Washington D.C. Significantly, Brian's name did not appear on any of these properties. The state of Massachusetts posited that Brian wanted out of the marriage and sought to retain his wife's wealth, opting for murder over divorce.

The state's case against Brian Walshe was fortified by a haunting piece of history. Nearly a decade before Ana went missing, she had reported Brian to the police for threatening to kill her and a friend. Despite the severity of this threat, the case was closed when Ana refused to cooperate with the prosecution. She later married Brian in 2015 and had three children with him.

The accumulated evidence painted a grim picture of a man driven by greed and capable of extreme violence. The state's case, robust in its incriminating details, offered little solace to those mourning Ana and seeking justice for her untimely and tragic disappearance.

Dee Ann Warner

Dee Ann Warner was a woman of many talents and roles: a loving wife, a caring sister, a doting grandmother, and an energetic businesswoman. However, to her daughter Raquel Bach, Dee Ann was first and foremost an amazing mother. Raquel fondly remembers a childhood filled with adventure and laughter, always buzzing with excitement alongside her adventurous mom. Their days were filled with joyful shopping trips and endless fun. Dee Ann's passion for shopping was infectious, turning regular days into exciting adventures.

The Warner family, who have been integral to their rural farming community in Franklin Township, Lenawee, Michigan, for five generations, were well-respected in the area. Greg, Dee Ann's brother, who was 18 years older than her, fondly remembers how she admired him, possibly even taking inspiration from him, especially in business. Greg, who prides himself on being a problem solver, sees some of his traits in Dee Ann. He admits that her stubborn independence sometimes led her to avoid asking for help.

With entrepreneurship in their bloodline, Dee Ann followed in the footsteps of her aunt and grandmother, both successful businesswomen. She made her mark in the male-dominated fields of trucking and agriculture, showing remarkable strength and determination. Her trucking business and other ventures were testaments to her resilience and respect in the industry.

But Dee Ann was not just a tough businesswoman; she was also known for her lively social presence. Raquel describes her mother as the life of the party, a person who effortlessly combined spunk, care, and compassion. Dee Ann had a remarkable ability to connect with people, making her a loved figure both personally and professionally. As a mother and grandmother, she was deeply devoted and loving.

However, the family's world turned upside down when Dee Ann suddenly disappeared. Her absence left a huge void, especially for her brother Craig, who couldn't reach her one chilling Sunday morning. This was unusual for them, given their close bond. The family's concern quickly grew, leading them to involve the police.

Raquel's worry intensified when she found out Dee Ann's youngest daughter, Angelina, wasn't with her. It was unlike Dee Ann to leave without Angelina, adding to the alarm. The family, once united by Dee Ann's vibrant energy, now found themselves in a desperate search for her, clinging to the hope of her safe return. This mysterious disappearance left everyone who knew her wondering: What could have happened to Dee Ann Warner, the vibrant heart of their family and community?

Her brother Greg found himself increasingly worried. He tried to get some clarity from her husband, Dale, but was left with more questions than answers. Greg couldn't hide his anxiety as he asked Dale, "What's happening, Dale?" The situation was baffling: Dee Ann had left behind her purse, phone, and even her curling iron, with all her vehicles still at home. Greg was puzzled – how could she have left without any of these things? Dale's guess that someone might have picked her up only added to the confusion.

Greg had known Dale since he married Dee Ann 15 years ago. They had both been in agricultural sales when Dee Ann and Dale met. Greg remembered bonding with Dale over work, but he always felt that their marriage was more about shared interests than deep love. He recalled their 2006 wedding in Saline, Michigan, as being more stylish than sentimental.

Dee Ann and Dale had blended their families from previous marriages, later welcoming their daughter, Angelina. Greg saw their marriage as a partnership, especially in business, like in their trucking company. But Raquel, Dee Ann's daughter from her first marriage, painted a different picture. She remembered tensions, particularly over business. Just a day before Dee Ann went missing, Raquel and her mother had a heart-to-heart. Dee Ann was at her limit and thinking of leaving Dale. Raquel wondered if selling the trucking business might save their marriage, but Dee Ann was clear: "It's too late for us," she had said. Raquel had never heard her mother speak so decisively about ending her marriage – a conversation that now haunted her.

On the Sunday Dee Ann vanished, her family was frantic. They combed the property and checked security footage, hoping for any clue. They looked for any unfamiliar cars that might have picked her up, but found nothing.

Realizing the severity of the situation, Raquel and her siblings felt they had to act. They persuaded Dale to report Dee Ann missing. Dissatisfied with Dale's plan to wait until the next morning, they went to Raquel's brother's house and called the police themselves to report Dee Ann missing.

The Lenawee County Sheriff's Office quickly started investigating Dee Ann's disappearance, looking into her last known contacts. They found out that the last people to see her were a family friend who had Angelina for the night and then her husband, Dale. However, the Sheriff's Office kept most details under wraps due to the ongoing nature of the case.

Greg, Dee Ann's brother, couldn't stop thinking about what might have happened to her. He was aware of the problems in her marriage, the intense arguments, and the overall toxic atmosphere. Initially, he even feared that Dee Ann might have been so overwhelmed that she considered harming herself. But after talking to experts and delving deeper, he ruled out this idea.

He became more and more convinced that Dee Ann had reached her limit with her troubled marriage to Dale and was planning to leave. He recalled that she had even told a friend about her plans to divorce.

In their search for answers, the family enlisted Billy Little, a well-known defense attorney and private investigator. Little, who had a background in capital murder cases and had worked for the U.S. Navy, took on the case not for money, but to genuinely help.

Once in Michigan, Little talked to over a hundred people. He found out that the day before she vanished, Dee Ann was ready to confront Dale and end their marriage, a decision she had shared with friends.

His investigation also revealed how deeply upset Dee Ann was. She was so distressed that she couldn't even sit still for a beauty appointment to get eyelash extensions, avoiding calls from Dale to keep her composure.

Despite the upheaval in her life, Dee Ann had made plans for future appointments, ones she would never make. Witnesses remembered how she seemed determined to avoid Dale, dismissing his call with a firm no.

This raised the question: had Dee Ann left to dodge the difficult conversation about divorce? Did she leave on her own? The family, after checking their home security footage, couldn't find any evidence to support this. Sheriff Troy Beever from Lenawee County, in a talk with Dateline, mentioned that neither their initial review nor the FBI's analysis of the footage provided clear answers about Dee Ann's fate.

In the wake of Dee Ann Warner's perplexing disappearance, her family, fueled by a blend of urgency and resolve, dove into an exhaustive search. They carefully combed through the security footage of their property, hoping to spot any hint of Dee Ann's last movements. They looked for any unknown vehicle that might have picked her up, but their efforts turned up no leads.

During this tense time, Dee Ann's husband, Dale, shared his account of the night leading up to her disappearance. His story was a mix of contradictions and revisions. Initially, he spoke of a severe argument they had, but later he downplayed its intensity. He described giving her a massage in the living room, where she fell asleep, and then moving her to the couch. According to Dale, that's where she spent the night, while he slept in another room. He claimed the last time he saw her was early in the morning, asleep on the couch.

Sheriff Bevere told Dateline in January about an intense argument involving Dee Ann, Dale, and some of her employees on the night before she vanished. This was a lead actively being pursued. Dale, meanwhile, had his own theories, wildly speculating that Dee Ann might be in Mexico, Jamaica, or even with another man in Australia, but these ideas seemed baseless as her passport remained unused.

As the seasons changed and Dee Ann remained missing, the community felt her absence deeply. The Lenawee County Fair, a beloved event for Dee Ann and her daughter Raquel, passed without her. They had shared many special moments there, from showing animals to enjoying funnel cakes. As fall arrived, painting Illinois County with vibrant colors, the community was overshadowed by a sense of loss, the mystery of Dee Ann's disappearance casting a shadow over the festive season.

Despite extensive searches of Dee Ann and Dale's property in late October 2021, nothing was found. By March, the investigation had intensified. The Lenawee County Sheriff's Office, joined by the Michigan State Police and the FBI, conducted thorough searches using aerial scans, dogs, ground-penetrating radar, and forensics. They delved into Dee Ann's medical records, finances, and social media, but the only discovery was a set of her keys.

Billy Little, leading an independent investigation, had a grim perspective. He doubted that Dee Ann would be found, dead or alive. Despite using advanced technology and extensive searches over thousands of acres, no significant evidence was uncovered, even in the areas around the office, business, trucking company, and fertilizer company.

The pressing question remained: If Dee Ann was harmed, where could she be? Despite the dim outlook, Little continued his search, driven by the family's wish to give Dee Ann a dignified farewell.

Looking back, Raquel remembers a haunting comment her mother made about her stepfather, Dale. This memory became even more significant after her mother's disappearance. Dee Ann had once shared with Raquel her fears about Dale, influenced by the true crime stories she watched on Dateline. She worried that Dale might do something extreme. In January 2022, when Dateline asked Sheriff Bevere about potential suspects, he kept an open mind, not ruling anyone out. The investigation into Dee Ann Warner's disappearance continued, casting a wide net in search of answers.

In the complex case of Dee Ann Warner's vanishing, Billy Little's independent investigation plays a crucial role. He faces a grim reality: there has been no sign that Dee Ann is alive. This harsh truth has led Greg, Dee Ann's caring and determined older brother, to the heart-wrenching belief that she might not be alive. Despite not finding her body, Greg's commitment to finding the truth is unwavering. He has put up significant cash rewards, tirelessly followed leads, and explored every possibility to uncover what happened to his sister.

Greg is relentlessly driven by the love for his sister and the desire for closure for his family. He clings to the hope that the truth will eventually come to light and bring some peace to those who miss Dee Ann.

The impact of this mystery extends beyond Greg. Dee Ann's daughter, Raquel, and her granddaughter, Angelina, both struggle with the deep loss they feel from Dee Ann's absence. The community also mourns the loss of a woman who was a dynamic part of their lives.

The family continues their plea for help in their quest to find Dee Ann. They share her description, hoping someone, somewhere might have seen her or know something about her disappearance. Dee Ann is 5 feet 4 inches tall, around 135 pounds, with brown hair and blonde highlights.

As time passes and the seasons change, the mystery of Dee Ann Warner's disappearance lingers, casting a shadow of sorrow and uncertainty over her family and community. But amidst this darkness, Greg's unwavering search for the truth and the community's support keep hope alive. They hold onto the belief that someday, they will understand what happened to Dee Ann and find a way to properly honor her memory.

Jason Jolkowski

I n Grand Island, Nebraska, a boy named Jason Jolkowski was born on a sunny day in June 1981. His parents, Kelly Murphy and Jim Jolkowski, watched with pride and love as their son grew, navigating the world with a unique blend of challenges and gifts. Jason, despite grappling with a learning disability that made speech and language a labyrinthine journey for him, possessed a mind that sparkled with brilliance, particularly when it came to the world of sports.

His intelligence shone through in unexpected ways, most notably in his encyclopedic knowledge of sports trivia. Jason's mother, Kelly, once shared on The Unfound Podcast a fascinating facet of her son's personality: "He was like a walking sports encyclopedia. You could ask him who won the World Series in 1953, and he'd have the answer at the tip of his tongue." It was a talent that left many in awe, underscoring the fact that intelligence takes many forms and often surprises us.

Jason, a shy and introspective young man, preferred the company of a close-knit circle of friends. He steered clear of the temptations that often ensnare the youth, such as drugs and alcohol, instead finding solace and joy in the warmth of his family. Standing tall at 6 feet 1 inch, with a slender build, brown hair, and deep brown eyes, he was a figure that combined physical presence with a gentle demeanor.

After graduating from Benson High School, Jason took on a part-time job at

Fazoli's, a local Italian fast-food joint, while pursuing his studies at Iowa Western Community College. It was here, in the realm of academia, that Jason embarked on a path that surprised many, including his mother Kelly. He chose to major in radio broadcasting, a field that seemed at odds with his quiet nature and his challenges with speech and comprehension.

But Jason was full of surprises. At college, he started to craft a new identity, one that would soon find its voice on the college radio station. Kelly recalls a memorable incident from one of his early broadcasts, where a prolonged silence had her worried that he might be struggling with the equipment. But soon, Jason's voice filled the airwaves, confidently and eloquently, marking the emergence of a new persona, vastly different from the reserved teenager his high school peers knew.

Jason's transformation was remarkable. On the air, he was dynamic, engaging, and charismatic—a complete 180-degree turn from his usual self. He quickly garnered a following, his voice becoming a familiar and beloved presence to his listeners. Jason Jolkowski had found his calling, his passion, and his voice.

The future seemed bright and full of promise for Jason, especially as late June 2001 approached. He was eagerly anticipating the start of a new job at a local radio station, a dream opportunity that would allow him to showcase his talents to a wider audience. His hard work and perseverance were paying off, and it felt like the beginning of something truly special.

However, fate had a different plan. On the morning of June 13, 2001, a phone call shattered the normalcy of the Jolkowski household. The phone's persistent ring echoed through the home, a sound that Jason responded to with his usual promptness. On the other end of the line was his boss from Fazoli's, urgently requesting Jason to come in early. Hesitation flickered in Jason's thoughts as he pondered his options. With his car unavailable, he considered the long walk to work but decided to seek a ride from a coworker instead.

The morning of June 13, 2001, unfolded with a sense of normalcy in the Jolkowski household, a calm before an unforeseen storm. Jason, always known for his poor sense of giving directions, had arranged a ride with a local coworker. They decided to meet at a place familiar and significant to both: Benson High School. This was their alma mater, a place etched with memories, standing stoically on Maple Street in Omaha, Nebraska, just a short 8-block walk from Jason's home. That route, traversed by Jason countless times, was as familiar to him as the rhythmic beating of his heart. It was a path so well-trodden that even the residents peering from the houses lining the street might recognize the lanky figure of Jason, a familiar presence in their daily vista.

On this particular day, Jason and his coworker had agreed to meet at 11 am. Aware of the time it would take to reach the high school, Jason spent his last moments at home wrapping up chores. His brother Michael and a neighbor recall seeing Jason performing the mundane yet comforting task of returning garbage cans from the curb to their place in the garage. With the familiar red Fazoli's t-shirt in hand, he set out, unwittingly embarking on a walk that would etch his name into the annals of mystery.

As the clock inched towards 11:15 am, Jason's coworker, waiting at the high school, began to feel the pangs of impatience. By 11:30 am, her worry had escalated. Concerned and puzzled, she exited her vehicle, her mind swirling with questions and apprehensions. She found a phone at a nearby gas station and dialed the Jolkowski residence. Initially, Michael, Jason's brother, answered, playfully impersonating Jason. However, sensing the urgency and concern in the coworker's voice, he quickly abandoned his jest. The realization that Jason hadn't reached the designated meeting spot sent a ripple of concern through Michael. He informed her that Jason had left home more than half an hour ago, implying that he should have arrived by then.

The coworker, now deeply troubled, made another call, this time to her boss at Fazoli's, explaining the situation. She was instructed to return to work, leaving the mystery of Jason's whereabouts hanging in the air like a dense fog.

His family reported him missing 24 hours after he was last seen. This delay, in adherence to the then-common "waiting period" before declaring someone missing, might have inadvertently let crucial initial hours slip away. At first, the police considered the possibility that Jason might have run away, which led to a delay in launching a formal investigation. It wasn't until 10 days after Jason vanished that the police began to seriously probe into his disappearance, a delay that many believe could have caused vital evidence and leads to slip through the cracks.

The investigation that unfolded was meticulous yet frustrating. Jason's coworker, the last person known to have planned to meet him, was thoroughly interviewed and subsequently cleared of any involvement. Authorities combed through security footage from the expanse of Benson High School, but it only confirmed the unsettling truth: Jason never made it to the school that day.

The circumstances surrounding his disappearance were baffling. Up to the moment he left his home, everything about Jason's behavior seemed normal, routine. He had completed his daily chores, left all his personal belongings behind, and it's believed he had no more than $60 in his pocket. His bank account, with $650 untouched, remains a silent testament to his abrupt vanishing. His car, untouched in the garage; his cell phone and ATM card, unused; his final paychecks from Fazoli's, unclaimed – all these details paint a picture of a sudden and unplanned disappearance. The question that haunts everyone is: What happened to Jason Jolkowski?

Over the years, various theories have surfaced, attempting to piece together the puzzle of Jason's fate. One prevailing theory suggests that Jason may have been the victim of a hit-and-run accident during his walk to the high school. This theory branches into multiple scenarios, each raising more questions than answers. Could it be that Jason, momentarily stepping off the sidewalk, was struck by a passing vehicle? Such a tragic accident could have left him severely injured or even lifeless. In a state of panic, the driver might have acted in one of two ways: either rushing an injured Jason to a hospital with intentions to help or, in a darker turn of events, removing his lifeless body from the scene to avoid consequences.

Another angle to this theory speculates that Jason, if he survived the accident, might have walked away with amnesia, losing all recollection of his past life. This notion, while less grim, leaves an open-ended question about his current whereabouts and well-being.

The perplexing disappearance has given rise to various theories, each attempting to make sense of the baffling circumstances that surround that fateful day. One such theory revolves around the possibility of a hit-and-run accident occurring between 10:45 am and 11:15 am. However, this theory raises the question of witnesses. Car accidents, especially in a city like Omaha, rarely go unnoticed. They're often accompanied by commotion, not just from the impact, but from the ensuing chaos and panic. Despite this, during the initial and subsequent police investigations, no one came forward to report such an incident. This silence from potential witnesses casts doubt on the hit-and-run theory.

Another set of theories speculates that Jason either took his own life or ran away. However, these theories lack substantial evidence and are largely speculative. From a family perspective, Jason was perceived as a happy, goal-oriented individual. He had a promising future ahead, particularly with his upcoming job as a local radio broadcaster. His newfound persona in the broadcasting world seemed to be a source of joy and fulfillment for him. His family also points to his strong religious beliefs and the absence of any apparent signs of depression to dispute the theory of suicide. Yet, we must consider that sometimes, even the happiest individuals can harbor deep personal struggles, often unbeknownst to those around them.

One critical argument against the theory of suicide is the absence of Jason's body. In a city as large as Omaha, it seems unlikely that his body would remain undiscovered if he had taken his own life. Similarly, the theory of Jason being a runaway also has its flaws. It's hard to imagine how far he could have gone with just $60, and if he had managed to travel further, it seems improbable that there would be no trace of him in today's digital and heavily surveilled world. The thought of Jason starting a new life under a new identity, completely avoiding social media and leaving his family in anguish, seems far-fetched.

The theory I find most plausible involves an element of trust and betrayal. Was Jason abducted? Could it be that during his walk to Benson High School, he encountered someone – either a stranger or an acquaintance – who offered him a ride? Picture Jason walking along his familiar route, when a vehicle slows down beside him. Maybe the driver strikes up a conversation, which leads to the offer of a ride. Or perhaps the driver is someone Jason knows – a family acquaintance or a friend. This person calls out to Jason, offering a ride to Fazoli's. Under the pressure of the moment and recognizing a familiar face, Jason might have accepted the offer, a decision that tragically altered the course of his life.

Jason's family, along with many others, believe that foul play is a likely explanation for his disappearance. Considering the area where Jason vanished, law enforcement officials took the possibility of abduction seriously. They interviewed multiple sex offenders in the vicinity and even conducted a search of one individual's home. However, these extensive efforts yielded no concrete evidence linking any of these individuals to Jason's disappearance. This lack of evidence only deepens the mystery, leaving us to ponder the various possibilities of what might have happened to Jason Jolkowski on that June morning.

Kelli Cribbs Abad

Kelli Cribbs' early life unfolded in the charming, rural setting of Brooklet, a short distance from the historic allure of Savannah, Georgia. Her childhood was a blend of simplicity and happiness, typical of life in a small town. Her days were bright with laughter and exploration under the expansive skies, and she found comfort in the presence of her brother and half-sister in their cozy family home.

Her parents, embodying the hardworking ethos typical of rural America, worked relentlessly on their small farm. Their long days and hardworking hands were evidence of their commitment to their family's well-being. Kelli, inheriting their strong work ethic, often helped with farm chores. She developed a love for the farm animals and enjoyed the simple pleasures of rural life. Her interests were diverse, including fishing, a pastime that reflected the patience and determination she saw in her parents.

As she grew, Kelli's heart was drawn to helping others, especially the elderly in her community. Spending time with her grandmother deeply influenced her outlook on life. These moments, filled with stories from the past and elderly wisdom, ignited Kelli's caring nature.

Despite a 14-year age difference, Kelli and her half-sister, Jennifer Lisa Schumann, shared a close and loving bond. Their conversations, whether in person or over the phone, were warm and familiar, typical of sibling relationships. Jennifer often spoke fondly of Kelli's ever-present smile, which brightened their lives.

Kelli's mother, Janice, remembered her daughter's sociable personality. "She always extended a helping hand, naturally connecting with both young and old," Janice reminisced. It came as no surprise to those who knew Kelli that she pursued a career in nursing and medical assistance, where her inherent compassion and empathy could truly flourish.

Kelli's life then intersected with Vince Abad, an airman at a nearby U.S. Air Force base. Their romance, rooted in Georgia, led to marriage in 2006. Married life for Kelli and Vince was a blend of love, commitment, and adaptation, as they moved to various Air Force bases. The couple welcomed two children, Vince and Kyrie, bringing new joy and challenges. Kelli's small stature posed complications during her pregnancies, but her resilience ensured the healthy birth of both children.

In 2008, Vince's military career led the family to a new life at Kadena Air Force Base in Okinawa, Japan. Kelli, ever positive, prepared for their new adventure on the subtropical island. They opted to live on-base, quickly forming connections and becoming part of the community there.

As time passed, however, their marriage encountered difficulties. Kelli confided in her family during a Skype call on October 25, 2011, about a potential move to either Germany or Alaska, hoping it might be a chance for a new beginning away from the troubles they were experiencing in Japan.

Seeking to overcome these challenges, Kelli and Vince, firm in their faith, turned to their pastor for guidance, aiming for reconciliation and healing.

The conversation on October 25th, sadly, was the last time Kelli's family would hear her voice. The following day, after a typical day with her children, including a church service where she and Vince sought to address their marital issues, Kelli inexplicably disappeared.

Vince later told Kelli's sister, Jennifer, about that night. He stayed at church for a discussion with the pastor after Kelli and the children had left. When he got home around 10 pm, the house was quiet, the children asleep, but Kelli was nowhere to be seen, and her car was gone. This raised immediate concerns among the family.

Kelli's mother, Janice, initially hoped Kelli might be at a friend's, but this seemed unlikely given Kelli's dedication as a mother. Jennifer and others who knew Kelli agreed that it was not like her to leave her children alone.

With no sign of Kelli by morning, Vince informed Kadena officials and local Japanese authorities. Kelli had previously stayed with friends after arguments, but this absence quickly became alarming.

Adding to the mystery, Kadena Air Force Base officials stated in a 2011 email that Kelli was seen entering the base at 8:37 pm on October 26th and leaving about 30 minutes later. Her phone, switched off that night, gave no further clues.

Three days later, on October 29th, Kelli's car was found near Cape Zampa's cliffs. The car contained her keys, phone, ID, and wedding rings, along with a note that seemed like a farewell, expressing love for her family and children. Jennifer, seeing the note, doubted its genuineness, convinced her sister would never abandon her children or consider suicide.

The perplexing case of Kelli's disappearance was further complicated by the absence of any writing tools in her abandoned car. Janice, Kelli's mother, was adamant that Kelli would have shared any significant marital issues with her. The family's frustration grew due to the slow and limited communication from the Air Force Office of Special Investigations (OSI).

The investigation, a collaboration between the Okinawa Police Department and the U.S. Air Force, was ongoing. However, jurisdictional complexities in Okinawa hampered progress. American bases operated under U.S. law with their own emergency and investigative services, but outside these bases, Japanese laws prevailed. This division of jurisdiction, further complicated by Okinawa's regional structure, added layers of complexity to the investigation.

Okinawa, with its rich history and cultural diversity, has long experienced mixed sentiments regarding the American military presence. The relationship between the local and American communities has been a blend of positive contributions and occasional tensions. Kelli's disappearance as an American in Japan contributed to this already complex dynamic.

Despite some challenges, many Americans in Okinawa have engaged in community efforts, from social work to environmental clean-ups, striving to positively integrate into Okinawan society. However, incidents like Kelli's disappearance can overshadow these efforts, sometimes leading to a generalized apprehension among the locals.

The involvement of various investigative agencies, each with its distinct procedures and jurisdiction, seemed to complicate the case further. This situation led to a sense of bureaucratic buck-passing, deepening the anguish and frustration for Kelli's family.

Driven by a mother's unyielding will, Janice traveled to Okinawa in November 2011. She tirelessly searched the island, distributing flyers and seeking any clue about her daughter's whereabouts. Janice firmly believed Kelli was taken against her will, a belief shared by those close to Kelli.

In an unexpected development, Vince remarried in 2014. This decision, made while Kelli was still missing, attracted scrutiny and raised questions among those following the case.

Journalists like Matt Burke from 'Stars and Stripes' and Jeff Smith, a former Marine now living in Okinawa, found themselves deeply involved in the perplexing case of Kelli's disappearance. Despite their efforts to uncover information and organize searches, they frequently encountered setbacks, reflecting the same frustrations Kelli's family faced.

The clues surrounding Kelli's case, such as her car exiting the base on the night she vanished, and its later discovery at Cape Zampa, a renowned tourist destination, only deepened the mystery. The location of the car near the cliffs at low tide hinted at a tragic scenario, but without conclusive evidence, various theories and speculations persisted.

Questions arose about whether Kelli could have ended up in the water, perhaps carried away into the rugged coastline's caves and gullies. The timing of her presumed disappearance and the subsequent finding of her car, both coinciding with low tide, challenged the idea that she may have jumped from the cliffs, as she would more likely have landed on the rocky shore rather than in the water.

The reluctance of the Office of Special Investigations (OSI) to release footage of Kelli's car leaving the base to her immediate family raised questions. This footage could potentially confirm whether Kelli was the one driving that night. The appearance of her car at Cape Zampa, nearly three days after she was last seen, added further complexity. Betty, an American photographer, noted the absence of Kelli's car at Cape Zampa late on the Friday night before it was found, introducing more uncertainty about who drove the car there.

The investigation was further complicated by the discovery of an unidentified adult fingerprint in the car. The car, found unlocked with Kelli's belongings and a brief note inside, presented a contradictory scenario. Considering Cape Zampa's known high-crime rate, the undisturbed state of Kelli's car, left for nearly three days, was highly unusual.

The distinctive identification of American vehicles in Okinawa, often targeted by thieves, made the undisturbed state of Kelli's car, especially in a high-crime area, even more puzzling.

Jeff's involvement in the case added another dimension. He received information from an airman about skeletal remains found in a remote part of northern Okinawa, far from Cape Zampa. However, this lead remained unexplored due to the lack of precise location and verifiable evidence.

Okinawa's history, characterized by rugged coastlines and caves used for various purposes over time, could theoretically provide explanations for unexpected findings like skeletal remains.

As time passes, the investigation into Kelli's disappearance continues, with local police asserting that the case remains open and active. Jeff persists in his search for the truth, while Kelli's family, particularly her mother Janice, holds onto the hope of finding Kelli and bringing her home. Janice's words, "I just want to find her and bring her home," resonate with a mother's enduring love and an unwavering desire for closure.

Ebby Steppach

On a serene spring day, March 31st, 1997, a new chapter began in the quaint suburbs of Little Rock, Arkansas. Ebby, a name that would soon resonate with vibrancy and spirit, was born to Laurie Jurnigan and Peter Steppach. In the heart of a close-knit community, Ebby's early years were woven with the threads of familial love and a deep connection to her roots.

As Ebby journeyed through her childhood, her family expanded, welcoming her older brother, Trevor, and later, their younger sister, Harris. Together, they painted a picture of sibling camaraderie, often found in the warm embrace of their grandparents' home or within the hallowed halls of their local church. The Steppach family was known for their artistic flair, a trait that permeated through their home and lives. In this creatively nurturing environment, Ebby discovered her passion for photography, a medium through which she expressed her unique view of the world.

As she blossomed into a teenager, Ebby's interests evolved, gravitating towards the pulsating world of trendy fashion. She skillfully intertwined her love for beauty with her artistic inclinations, delving into the realms of cosmetology. Ebby was a natural, quickly mastering the art of hairstyling and makeup, transforming these skills into a beloved hobby.

High school brought introspection and dreams for Ebby. She envisioned a future where she could weave her passion for beauty and business, aspiring to become both a cosmetologist and a real estate agent. But Ebby's aspirations weren't just career-driven; she harbored a profound empathy for those around her. She became a guardian angel to her peers, often stepping in to shield her loved ones from harm. Her acts of kindness and her tireless efforts to uplift those in need left an indelible mark on her community.

However, beneath her compassionate exterior, Ebby was fiercely independent. As she neared adulthood, she began to chart her own course, relying on her wisdom and intuition rather than seeking approval from others. This independence, while admirable, began to create ripples in her life during the summer before her senior year. Eager to spread her wings, Ebby transferred from her private school to Little Rock Central High School, a decision that marked the beginning of a transformative phase in her life.

During this time, Ebby also embarked on a new journey, joining the team at a Foot Locker store in McCain Mall. It was a period of change, not just in her career but also in her personal life. Her mother, Laurie, who had since experienced the ebbs and flows of life with a divorce and remarriage, noticed a shift in Ebby's demeanor. Ebby, once the rule-abiding daughter, started to challenge the boundaries, often staying out late and attending local parties. Her parents wondered if these changes were influenced by her new relationship, which Laurie viewed with concern, feeling that the boy was leading Ebby astray.

The family dynamics became strained, and Ebby's spirit of independence ultimately led her to move out of her parents' home. She sought solace and freedom, splitting her time between her grandparents' home, her brother Trevor's place, and the homes of friends. One such friend, Danielle, noticed Ebby's internal struggles. Danielle recalled how Ebby would often seek refuge in long, midnight drives, with music as her only companion. These nocturnal escapades provided temporary solace, but the root of Ebby's turmoil remained a mystery.

As senior year progressed, Ebby's attendance at school waned. Then, on October 24th, 2015, everything came to a head. Ebby returned home, distraught, revealing to her mother and step-father that she had been assaulted at a party. She was adamant that the incident had been recorded and demanded justice. Shortly after this revelation, Ebby left in a whirlwind of emotions, her communication with family and friends becoming increasingly erratic and concerning.

The following day, October 25th, Ebby made a haunting phone call to her brother, her words cryptic and filled with regret. After that call, Ebby vanished, leaving a void in the hearts of all who knew her. Her disappearance cast a shadow over Little Rock, leaving unanswered questions and a community in distress. It wasn't until May 2018, two and a half years later, that the tragic resolution came to light. The remains of Ebby Steppach were discovered in Chalamont Park, turning her missing person's case into a cold homicide investigation, a mystery that lingers in the minds of those who loved her and the community that still seeks answers.

In the transformative summer of 2015, Ebby's life took a dramatic turn, painting her days with shades of change and uncertainty. She embarked on a new journey, joining the workforce at a local Foot Locker, a job that symbolized her growing independence. This period also marked the beginning of a relationship, one that her mother Laurie and stepfather Michael viewed with concern, sensing it wasn't in her best interest.

Ebby's quest for autonomy didn't stop there. She made the bold decision to leave the comfort of her parent's home and explore new academic horizons by enrolling in a public school for her senior year. But with these changes came a noticeable shift in her demeanor. Ebby's once calm and collected nature gave way to signs of agitation, both in her personal life and social interactions. Her attendance at school began to falter, a stark contrast to her previous academic record. She started skipping classes, leaving those who cared about her puzzled and concerned.

This pattern of truancy reached its peak on a seemingly ordinary Wednesday, October 21st. Danielle, a close friend who had become Ebby's confidante and support, texted her about being late due to a doctor's appointment. She suggested that Ebby could leave school on her own if needed. Ebby's response was nonchalant yet tinged with mystery, hinting at "drama" she didn't wish to face that day. Danielle, unaware of the specifics, could only speculate about what was troubling Ebby.

Despite these undercurrents of turmoil, the friends managed to spend a pleasant evening together later that day. However, the calm was short-lived. On the night of Friday, October 23rd, Ebby attended a party solo, a gathering unfamiliar to Danielle and seemingly known only to Ebby. It was at this party that Ebby's life took a darker turn. She was assaulted by four men, a horrific act allegedly captured on one of their cellphones.

The following morning, Ebby, in a state of distress, returned to her mother's home. She revealed the harrowing details of the assault to Laurie and Michael and insisted on reporting the crime to the police. Her parents, deeply concerned, agreed to meet her at the police station later that day. But before heading to the station, Ebby felt compelled to visit her brother Trevor, wanting to reassure him amidst her prolonged absence.

Ebby's day continued with a visit to her grandparents' home, where she sought a brief respite by watching television and sharing a meal, followed by a light-hearted outing for frozen yogurt. Around 8 p.m., she left her grandparents, mentioning plans to meet Michael, which contrasted her earlier statement to Danielle. As the evening turned to night, Laurie and Michael grew increasingly worried, unable to reach their daughter.

Their concerns escalated when Michael theorized that Ebby might have gone in search of the incriminating cellphone video on her own. Cellphone records later revealed that Ebby had sent multiple texts to the men she accused of assaulting her at the party. The following afternoon, a disoriented call from

Ebby to Trevor only deepened the mystery. She claimed to be outside his house, but Trevor found no sign of her. When pressed for her location, Ebby's responses were vague and confused, ending with a cryptic admission of a mistake before the call abruptly ended.

As Sunday night enveloped the town, Ebby's parents reported her missing. The police, adhering to department procedures, waited 12 hours after her last known contact to officially begin their investigation. Meanwhile, a frantic Danielle scoured the town, desperately seeking any clue to her friend's whereabouts.

Three days after the chilling phone call, a security guard made a startling discovery in Chalamont Park – Ebby's 2003 Volkswagen Passat, abandoned in a parking lot near a wooded area. The car remained untouched for two days before law enforcement conducted a thorough search. Inside, they found Ebby's phone, wallet, and contact lenses, with the car's gas tank empty, the battery dead, and the key still in the ignition.

As the days turned into weeks and months, the search for Ebby Steppach continued with unwavering intensity. The mystery deepened and concern grew among those who knew her. In a poignant display of dedication, Ebby's close friend, Kayleigh, and her mother, Margie Foley, took it upon themselves to scour the areas surrounding Chalamont Park. During one of their searches, they encountered a disturbing and unmistakable odor of decomposition near a sewage drain. Driven by concern and the hope of finding any clue, they promptly alerted the Little Rock Police Department.

Despite their earnest appeals, the response from the detectives assigned to Ebby's case was disheartening. The authorities, having previously combed the area with cadaver dogs, dismissed the Foleys' discovery, attributing the smell to animal remains rather than human. The Foleys, though disheartened, were not deterred in their quest for answers.

As the calendar turned to November, Ebby's family, fueled by a blend of hope and desperation, publicly implored the community for assistance. They announced a $3,000 reward for any information that could lead to Ebby, igniting a new wave of volunteer efforts. In April 2016, a concerted search and rescue operation explored the woods near Markham Street and Bowman Road, yet, frustratingly, nothing significant was uncovered.

The persistence of the investigators and the community never waned. In November 2016, police conducted an extensive three-day search in Chalamont Park, the site of earlier suspicions, but again, no clues emerged. By May 2017, the grim reality began to set in. Authorities started to theorize that Ebby's case was likely a homicide. In response, the Steppach family, determined to find the truth, increased their reward for information to $50,000.

Seeking new perspectives, in October 2017, the Steppach family enlisted the expertise of private investigator TJ Ward, known for his involvement in the Natalie Holloway case. This move brought international attention to Ebby's disappearance, further highlighted when Dr. Phil interviewed Laurie and Trevor Steppach in December 2017.

The case, which had seemed to be at a standstill, suddenly gained momentum in May 2018. A new search operation in Chalamont Park led to a harrowing discovery – skeletal remains were unearthed from a drainage pipe. The remains were swiftly sent for forensic analysis, and soon, the devastating confirmation came: they were the remains of Ebby Steppach.

In October 2018, marking three years since Ebby's mysterious disappearance, law enforcement shared a significant but guarded update. The medical examiner had determined a preliminary cause of death, but the details were withheld from the public. The investigation was ongoing, classified as an open homicide case.

Delving into the intricate web of Ebby Steppach's case, it becomes evident that while there may not be glaring, obvious clues or substantial leads, there lies a subtle yet potentially crucial piece of the puzzle in the finer details. One specific area that beckons for a closer examination is Ebby's cell phone records. These records, like hidden chapters of a story, hold the potential to reveal critical interactions and insights into the final days before her disappearance, as well as shed light on the early investigative missteps.

A pivotal moment in the case emerged from a series of text messages sent by Ebby from her phone to several men implicated in a sexual assault at a party on Friday, October 23rd. These messages, unearthed by Monty Vickers, the first private investigator hired by the Steppach family, depicted Ebby in a confrontational stance, threatening to involve the police. The ambiguity in her messages – whether she sought to erase the alleged video or to press for cooperation – remains a question. Yet, these texts might be more telling than they appear at first glance. They could align with the final, unsettling phone call Ebby had with her brother on Sunday, October 25th. If the texts provoked a threatening response, they could explain the fear and regret in Ebby's voice during that call, culminating in her saying she "messed up" before the abrupt end of the conversation.

Regrettably, the police investigation did not delve into these texts or the last phone call to trace the cell towers for potential locations. The absence of this crucial data leaves a gap in understanding the context and location of these pivotal communications. Should this data ever be analyzed, it could illuminate the path Ebby took and the people she interacted with, offering invaluable insights into the case.

Another bewildering aspect arises from the cell phone records – two mysterious calls made from Ebby's phone to the Little Rock Police Department on the night of Saturday, October 24th. Recorded as outgoing calls, each roughly a minute long, these calls are believed by the Steppach family to be Ebby's attempts to report the assault. However, in a perplexing twist, these calls seem to have left no trace within the Little Rock Police Department. Journalist

Jenny Monk notes that the officers claimed no record of these calls – no notes, no call logs. This not only reflects a disconcerting lack of documentation but also casts a shadow of suspicion over the LRPD. How could consecutive calls from a young woman reporting an assault, or expressing fear about her situation, be completely overlooked? Was it a case of miscommunication, or did the authorities dismiss it as inconsequential?

Without concrete evidence of these calls from the police's end, the true nature of Ebby's phone interactions remains shrouded in mystery. The lack of clarity on why she called and what she communicated only fuels concerns about the initial handling of her case.

In the early stages of the investigation, when Ebby Steppach was considered a missing person rather than a homicide victim, a myriad of theories surfaced about her possible whereabouts and whether she had left of her own volition. Now, with the somber knowledge of her death and likely murder, many of these theories have lost their relevance. Yet, some online speculators still ponder if Ebby's tragic end could have been self-inflicted, a theory which emerges from her disoriented state during the last phone call with her brother, Trevor. They conjecture that in a moment of mental breakdown, she might have sought refuge in the sewer drain at Chalamont Park, either to escape her turmoil or evade someone pursuing her, leading to her untimely death. However, these theories hold little weight when scrutinized. The conditions in the enclosed space, the lack of any implements of self-harm, and the absence of evidence such as blood trails, make the suicide theory implausible. Additionally, had Ebby been stuck, it seems likely her cries for help would have been heard in the frequently visited park.

With the police treating Ebby's death as a homicide, the focus shifts from the question of how she died to who is responsible. Among the theories, one that has gained traction is the involvement of a serial killer, though a detailed examination of Arkansas's criminal history provides no clear links to such a pattern in Ebby's case. Despite the absence of a definitive serial killer connection, this possibility cannot be entirely dismissed, considering the unpredictable nature of such criminal behavior.

Another line of inquiry that has captured local interest is the potential role of gang activity in Ebby's disappearance and death. Little Rock's history with gang-related crimes, including assault, murder, and trafficking, raises the question of whether Ebby's changed behavior and associations in the months leading up to her disappearance might have inadvertently entangled her with dangerous elements. The haunting words she spoke in her last phone call, "I messed up," could potentially indicate a deeper entanglement with perilous circumstances than initially understood.

The most compelling and realistic theory, however, centers on the possibility that Ebby's death was connected to the four men she accused of sexually assaulting her. Despite the Little Rock Police Department initially dismissing these individuals as suspects, their direct involvement with Ebby before her disappearance and the potential motive to silence her make them key figures in the ongoing investigation. The lack of public identification of these men, coupled with rumors on internet forums about their connections, adds layers of complexity and intrigue to the case.

The handling of the investigation itself has been a subject of intense scrutiny and criticism. Key missteps by the original detectives, such as the dismissal of the foul odor reported near the park's drainage system and the delayed response to the abandoned Volkswagen, indicate a worrying lack of urgency and thoroughness. The failure to promptly interrogate key witnesses like Ebby's grandparents, the security guard who discovered her car, and the lack of preservation of crucial 911 call records further compound the perception of negligence in the investigation's early stages.

These oversights and the seeming indifference of the initial investigative team have not only hindered the progress of the case but also eroded public trust. The community's hope now lies with the current investigators, who are urged to re-examine these overlooked details and pursue all leads with the seriousness and diligence that Ebby's case deserves.

It's understandable, to an extent, why law enforcement would hold back information in an ongoing homicide investigation - to protect the integrity of the case, safeguard the victim's family, and prevent the perpetrator from gaining any advantage. However, this necessary discretion also fosters a breeding ground for community speculation and conspiracy theories. Unsubstantiated rumors, like the alleged involvement of a police officer's son, gain momentum in the volatile realm of the internet, further muddling the truth. The inability to confirm or refute these claims only adds to the frustration and uncertainty surrounding the case.

From our perspective, it seems likely that Ebby had a resolve fueled by courage when she left her grandparents' house on that fateful Saturday, October 24th. She appeared determined not to let the heinous actions of her assailants go unpunished. Ebby's mother, Laurie, has spoken of her daughter's forthright nature, especially when someone's safety was at stake. In this instance, Ebby stood up for herself, refusing to remain silent. She reached out to some of her attackers, threatening legal action and demonstrating her awareness of the video evidence. This bold move may have instilled fear and anger in the men she confronted.

It's plausible that the attackers, in a desperate bid to control the situation, feigned remorse and suggested a meeting under the guise of deleting the videos and offering an apology. Ebby, who Laurie suggests saw the best in people, might have naively agreed to meet, hoping for a peaceful resolution. Tragically, this meeting likely marked the point where things took a grim turn.

Chalamont Park, where Ebby's car was eventually found, may not have been the original meeting place but rather the location where her car was abandoned to mislead investigators and buy the perpetrators time. The initial police search of the park found no trace of Ebby, possibly because her body had been moved to the drainage pipe only later - a theory that aligns with the foul odor detected by the Foley family and the absence of any scent picked up by cadaver dogs during the initial search.

The frequency and specifics of any subsequent movements of Ebby's remains are uncertain. It's possible that the area where her remains were eventually discovered was not their initial resting place, adding another layer of complexity to the already baffling timeline of events.

As it stands, the true actions and involvement of the original detectives, the four men accused of assault, and any potential accomplices remain shrouded in mystery, pending further investigation and potential arrests. Until the case sees a breakthrough, all that remains is to honor Ebby's memory with the respect and dignity she deserves, keeping her story alive in the hope that justice will eventually be served.

Angela Whalen Hudson

Angela Whalen Hudson, affectionately known as Angie by those who cherished her, was a vibrant 33-year-old woman, a devoted wife, and a loving mother residing in the quiet, unincorporated area of Pelham, North Carolina. Nestled in Rockingham County and brushing against the Virginia border, Pelham was a place of rural tranquility and community spirit. Angela, however, was not a native of North Carolina; her roots traced back to the sun-soaked landscapes of Arizona. Despite this, Angela had a strong familial connection to North Carolina, which played a significant role in her decision to move there. It was a move driven by love and a sense of duty – to be closer to and support her family members who lived in the vicinity.

In Pelham, Angela found her calling in the world of childcare. She had a natural affinity for nurturing and caring for children, a passion that was more than just a job for her. Angela's sister often reminisced about how caring for children wasn't just Angela's profession, it was her passion, her life's work. This love for children led Angela to a career in a daycare environment, where she could make a meaningful impact on young lives every day.

Angela's life took a romantic turn when she met Robert. Their love story was one that led to marriage and Angela moving into their shared home in Pelham. This house, which later became the center of a perplexing mystery, was situated in a locale that was picturesque yet isolated – a home surrounded by dense forests, with a winding driveway that seemed to hide it from the prying eyes of the main road.

However, beneath this idyllic surface, Angela's life was threaded with complexities and challenges. In mid-August 2001, a crucial yet often overlooked detail emerged in Angela's story. She filed for and was granted an order of protection against Robert. This legal document painted a different picture of her domestic life, one that was fraught with difficulties. Under this order, Angela had the right to remain in the family home for up to a year, provided she secured new employment and a different place to live.

In a twist that seems almost unbelievable, Robert, who ran a contracting business from a workshop on the same property, was granted permission by the judge to access his workshop between 8 a.m. and 4 p.m. The proximity of these buildings – some estimates say 500 feet, others 200 – added a layer of complexity to Angela's situation. The property, even when viewed from satellite maps today, is engulfed in dense forestation. The workshop, hidden deeper within the property, could only be reached by passing the family home – a daily reminder of the troubled marriage Angela was trying to escape.

This tense coexistence was underscored by a chilling incident recounted by Angela's aunt, who stood by her side during the court proceedings. As they left the courthouse, having just secured the order of protection, Angela's husband ominously remarked, "You'll be out by Christmas." This statement, laden with foreboding, would later echo in the minds of all who knew Angela.

In a profound conversation that would later hold significant importance, Angela confided in her aunt, revealing a secret safeguard she had in place. She instructed her aunt that, should anything ever happen to her, she must seek out Angela's journals. These journals weren't ordinary; they were detailed accounts of the turbulent and distressing experiences Angela had with her husband, Robert. This vital piece of information, relayed by Angela's aunt, painted a picture of a woman who was meticulously documenting her life's struggles, perhaps as a means of seeking justice or understanding in the future.

Angela, determined to change the course of her life, had decided to file for divorce. On the morning of Thursday, September 20, 2001, she performed the routine act of walking her young children to the bus stop. These children, from a previous relationship, were not Robert's, and their regular routine was a comforting constant in their lives. That day, Angela had an appointment with an attorney – a significant step towards her new beginning. Tragically, she never made it to that appointment. According to official reports, the last person to claim to have seen her was her husband, Robert, at around 10:00 a.m. that day. Neighbors corroborated this, noting that Robert was the only person they observed entering or leaving the property.

The normalcy of that day shattered when Angela's children returned from school. They came home to a chilling silence and an unsettling scene – their mother's car parked outside, half-prepared food left abandoned on the counter as if Angela had been suddenly interrupted. Adding to the distress, the phone in the house was inoperable. The cause – whether due to severed lines, unpaid bills, or physically removed phones – remained a mystery. The children, confronted with their mother's inexplicable absence and no means to reach out for help, faced an unimaginable ordeal. Their only option was to turn to Robert, the very man their mother feared deeply, evidenced by the order of protection she had against him. When asked about Angela's whereabouts, Robert's vague response was that she had "gone somewhere."

As the sun rose on Friday, the sense of unease grew. Angela had plans for dinner with her aunt that evening, but all attempts to contact her were futile. The aunt, sensing something amiss, especially with the phone line, reached out to the Rockingham County Sheriff's Office for a welfare check. The officers arrived to find Angela's children alone in the house, the phone line disabled, and Robert casually in his workshop.

The investigation into Angela's disappearance was rife with complexities and ambiguities. According to the official narrative, Angela had reportedly told a "family member" that she was going somewhere. However, this information came from Robert, the very person from whom Angela sought protection. This detail was taken at face value, shaping the narrative of Angela's disappearance. Posters and missing-person reports suggested that Angela had willingly left, abandoning her children, her glasses, medication, purse, jewelry, clothes, and car. This narrative, built around Robert's account, painted Angela as an irresponsible mother who had chosen to disappear.

Upon hearing the bewildering news of Angie's vanishing, her sisters, propelled by a mix of anxiety and determination, flew in from different states, converging in a united front to find their beloved sister. In their hearts, they carried a blend of hope and dread, clinging to the faint possibility that Angie might still be found. They quickly took charge of arranging care for Angie's children, ensuring their safety and stability in the midst of this unforeseen family crisis.

Angie's sisters engaged with the initial detectives on the case, hoping for a breakthrough or at least some guidance. However, they were met with a disheartening response. According to Angie's sister, the detectives casually suggested that Angie might have simply run away, a theory that mirrored the conclusion drawn in the case of Michelle Hundley Smith. This dismissive attitude left Angie's sisters not just perplexed but deeply frustrated. How could someone who loved her children and life just disappear voluntarily?

As they delved deeper into Angie's life, trying to piece together the puzzle of her disappearance, they encountered suspicious and alarming roadblocks. While gathering Angie's belongings from her house, they found certain areas off-limits, areas which a family member of Robert's physically barred them from accessing. One such area was a room containing a deep freezer; another was a part of the workshop that housed numerous saws. These restrictions only fueled their suspicions and raised agonizing questions. Why were these areas forbidden? What secrets did they hold?

The sisters managed to find some of Angie's journals. One contained poetry, a window into Angie's soul, while the other was curiously missing several pages, torn out, leaving gaping holes in what might have been crucial evidence or insights into her life and struggles.

Disturbed and desperate for answers, Angie's family reached out to one of the detectives on the case. They poured out their concerns and the peculiarities they'd encountered in Angie's home. The detective's response was noncommittal – a promise to look into it. However, years later, a haunting realization came to light. A newer detective, now overseeing the case, revealed there was no record of the family's earlier reports. Their efforts to aid the investigation, it seemed, had vanished into thin air, just like Angie.

The family learned that Robert had interacted with the authorities only a handful of times and had refused to take a polygraph test. The same family member who had restricted access to parts of Angie's property had, according to authorities, completely refused to cooperate with the investigation. These revelations only deepened the family's suspicions and their sense of helplessness.

To this day, Angie's family grapples with unanswered questions and a gnawing sense of injustice. Why was there no thorough search for Angie? Why were their earnest reports seemingly ignored? If something nefarious had happened to Angie, what was the point of an order of protection that failed to protect her?

Angela Whalen Hudson was 33 years old on that fateful day, September 20, 2001, when she vanished from her home in Pelham, North Carolina. Angie, a Caucasian woman, stood 5 feet 7 inches tall, weighed about 128 pounds, and had blonde hair and blue eyes. She was identifiable by her distinct tattoos: a red scorpion on her back, a Chinese dragon on her upper right shoulder, and Egyptian hieroglyphics on her right ankle. She also had a scar from a tubal ligation surgery on her abdomen. These physical details, etched in the memories of her loved ones, are poignant reminders of the vibrant, unique individual they continue to miss and seek.

52

Audrey Moran & Jonathan Reynoso

On a seemingly ordinary day, May 10, 2017, a series of events unfolded that would soon grip the hearts of many. Audrey Moran, a dedicated employee at Extra Space Storage in Bermuda Dunes, California, was going about her day, surrounded by the familiarity of her workplace. Little did she know, this day would mark the beginning of an enduring mystery.

Earlier in the day, Audrey had spent time with her boyfriend, Jonathan Reynoso, and his roommate, a casual gathering before she had to head off to work. Jonathan, meanwhile, had plans of his own. He claimed to be traveling to Brawley, California, accompanied by a group of friends - a seemingly innocuous trip that would later become a focal point of speculation and concern.

After her shift at Extra Space Storage, Audrey made a brief stop at her sister's home in Coachella, California. Contrary to initial reports that suggested she had visited her mother's house, it was later confirmed that her sister's residence was her actual destination. It was here, around 8:00 pm, that Audrey shared her plans to pick up Jonathan. He was returning from his Brawley trip and, without a car of his own, relied on Audrey for transportation. Though Audrey didn't disclose the exact location of their meeting, she mentioned she'd be dropping him off at his place in Palm Desert, California, afterwards.

A puzzling twist emerged at 8:45 pm that evening. Audrey's sister received a text message containing a photo of Audrey and Jonathan together. While it appeared to be an older photo, it misleadingly suggested that Audrey and Jonathan were currently together. This assumption, however, has never been verified. Authorities speculate the photo was sent simply as a playful gesture, and they don't suspect any foul play related to it.

The following day, May 11, 2017, alarm bells began to ring. Audrey's family, accustomed to her consistent communication, found it strange and worrisome when their calls and texts went unanswered. Concerned by this uncharacteristic silence, they reached out to her repeatedly, only to be met with a void of responses.

Realizing something was amiss, the Moran family took action. In the early hours of May 12, they reported Audrey missing to the Indio Police Department. This marked the beginning of an intensive investigation into the disappearances of both Audrey Moran and Jonathan Reynoso.

In the initial phase of what would soon become a deeply intriguing and heart-wrenching case, the Indio Police Department took the helm of the investigation into the disappearances of Audrey Moran and Jonathan Reynoso. At first, the situation was treated as a case of voluntary missing adults, largely because there were no immediate signs suggesting otherwise. However, this classification did little to ease the growing concern among their friends and family scattered throughout the Inland Empire in California.

Investigators delved into the lives of Audrey and Jonathan, interviewing those who knew them best. Friends, family members, colleagues - all were questioned in an effort to piece together the puzzle. Interestingly, everyone interviewed echoed a similar sentiment: there had been no apparent red flags in the couple's behavior prior to their disappearance. Described as having a healthy and happy relationship, the mystery of their vanishing seemed all the more baffling.

A particularly intriguing aspect of the case revolves around the people

Jonathan was reported to have traveled to Brawley with. To this day, it remains unclear if these individuals were ever interviewed by the authorities. Adding to the complexity, one of Jonathan's close friends reported receiving a message from him at approximately 9:05 pm on May 10, 2017, sent through a group Instagram chat - this would be one of the last known communications from him.

The case took a significant turn on the morning of May 12, 2017. Audrey's 2010 charcoal grey GMC Terrain SUV was discovered parked off westbound I-10, west of Oak Valley Parkway in Beaumont, California. This location was puzzlingly off-course, lying a considerable 45 minutes west of the route one would take to Brawley. The SUV, located with the help of On-Star tracking, showed no signs of forced entry or damage. It was in good working order, with a full gas tank, silently holding its secrets by the roadside.

In the aftermath of the vehicle's discovery, bloodhounds were brought in, a move that added yet another layer of mystery. While reports are mixed on whether the dogs picked up the scents of both Audrey and Jonathan or just Jonathan, what's certain is their ability to track a scent for about 20 yards westward from the SUV before it vanished abruptly. This intriguing detail led investigators to speculate that the pair might have transferred to another vehicle.

A thorough search of the SUV was conducted upon its arrival at the Indio Police Department. The search was meticulous, yet frustratingly, yielded no significant findings. Neither Audrey's purse nor Jonathan's wallet was found, and both their cellphones were missing. Forensic tests, too, turned up nothing unusual. The vehicle, having revealed no clues, was eventually returned to the Moran family.

The discovery of the SUV on I-10 opened up a myriad of questions about how and why the couple might have left the area. A crucial setback in the investigation was the realization that the interstate cameras, designed only for monitoring live traffic conditions, did not record footage, leaving a gaping hole in potential surveillance evidence. In light of this, the Moran family issued a public appeal, urging anyone in the lower Coachella Valley who might have seen the SUV, bearing the California license plate 6MIG265, in the week preceding the mysterious disappearance, to come forward with any information, however small it might seem.

The Moran and Reynoso families, united in their distress and determination, embarked on a poignant mission to keep the story of their loved ones in the public eye, hoping against hope for a breakthrough.

Jonathan's mother, Mayra Torres, was overcome with a sense of urgency when she learned of her son's disappearance. She immediately booked a flight to the area, a tangible expression of a mother's desperate need to be close to the search for her child. Together with other family members, they embarked on a remarkable campaign, distributing thousands of flyers adorned with the couple's photos. This labor of love and anxiety saw these flyers reaching corners far and wide – across southern California, Arizona, Mexicali, Nevada, and even in the trailer parks dotting Oak Valley Parkway. The families also turned to the power of social media, rallying support under the hashtag #FindJonathanandAudrey, a digital beacon of hope in their quest for answers.

As the investigation trudged on, the police expressed their belief that the critical window in the couple's disappearance lay between May 10 and May 11, 2017. They also posited that Audrey and Jonathan likely never made it to Jonathan's residence in Palm Desert, a troubling piece of the puzzle that only deepened the mystery.

The couple's cellphones, silent witnesses to their last known movements, offered scant clues. Cellphone pings indicated that neither Audrey nor Jonathan had made or received calls from outside the eastern Coachella Valley on the fateful night they vanished. The subsequent silence of their phones, which have not pinged off any other cell towers, suggested they either ran out of battery or were deliberately turned off shortly after they were last heard from.

In a curious twist, a pizza box found in Jonathan's residence cast doubt on whether he had actually journeyed to Brawley on May 10, 2017. The pizza, believed to have been delivered around 5:45 pm that evening, contradicted the timeline of his supposed out-of-town trip, especially given his lack of a vehicle. This puzzling detail left investigators grappling with questions and theories about his whereabouts that night. Despite their efforts, by 2019, they were still unable to confirm if Jonathan had indeed traveled to Brawley. The prevailing belief was that he might have been on his way back to Palm Desert with friends, but the identity of these friends remained shrouded in mystery.

In an effort to widen the net of information and gather new leads, the Indio Police Department reached out to law enforcement agencies across the country, harnessing tools like the National Law Enforcement Teletype System and the Missing Unidentified Person's System to amplify the reach of their search.

On May 25, 2017, the Moran family organized a prayer service at Our Lady Soledad Catholic Church in Coachella, a place imbued with sentimental significance as it was the very church where Audrey had been baptized. This poignant service, lasting an hour, drew a gathering of over 650 people, a testament to the impact of Audrey and Jonathan's story on the hearts of many.

Amidst this outpouring of communal support, the families also turned to fundraising efforts to aid in their search. A GoFundMe campaign was established, aiming to raise funds for a reward for information leading to the couple's whereabouts. Additionally, a fundraiser was held at La Quinta Brewing Co. on June 23, 2017. Their goal of $10,000 was eventually met.

The digital landscape became a breeding ground for theories and rumors, many revolving around the personal lives of the missing couple. This flood of information, while indicative of the public's deep interest and concern, posed a challenge for the investigators. Each rumor, each whisper of speculation, had to be meticulously checked for its relevance and accuracy, inadvertently slowing down the search process. In response to this, investigators have made earnest appeals to the public, urging them to focus on facts and refrain from spreading unverified rumors, to keep the integrity of the investigation intact.

Amidst this whirlwind of social media chatter, conflicting reports emerged about Audrey's personal life, specifically regarding whether she was seeing someone else while dating Jonathan. Their relationship, still in its nascent stages and not yet exclusive, became a subject of intense scrutiny. Adding to the complexity, a man believed to have had a past relationship with Audrey reported his car missing only to later set it ablaze. This incident, which occurred a few days after the couple went missing, led investigators to the burned vehicle near Thermal, an unincorporated community in the Coachella Valley. Although this man was interviewed by police and his home was subject to a search warrant, it remains unclear if any significant findings were made. To date, no concrete connection between this incident and the disappearances of Audrey and Jonathan has been established, leaving Audrey's SUV as the sole vehicle directly linked to their case.

In a heartfelt community effort, a fundraiser was organized at Stuft Pizza Bar & Grill in September 2017. The goal was to support the production of flyers, banners, and other materials crucial for keeping the search alive and the story in the public consciousness.

Remarkably, there has been no suspicious activity noted on the couple's financial records, adding yet another layer of mystery to their sudden vanishing.

In a strategic move to consolidate efforts and information, the case was handed over to the Riverside County Sheriff's Department Central Homicide

Unit. By January 2018, the investigators announced their belief that Audrey and Jonathan did not leave voluntarily, a revelation that only deepened the enigma surrounding their fate.

In a poignant display of hope and remembrance, family members distributed bracelets bearing the names of Audrey and Jonathan, along with a contact number for tips. This small yet significant gesture served as a constant reminder of their loved ones' plight and a call to action for anyone who might have information.

In 2019, the Riverside County Sheriff's Department expressed a steadfast belief that the cases were still solvable, despite the paucity of information released to the public. The investigation remained active, fueled by hope and the tireless dedication of investigators who have poured countless hours into the search. Numerous warrants have been issued, yet no individual has been publicly named as a suspect or a person of interest. The couple seems to have vanished without a trace, leaving behind no definitive clues as to their whereabouts or their fate, and no evidence to ascertain whether they are alive or deceased. As such, their cases continue to be treated as missing persons investigations.

One early theory suggested that the couple might have chosen to vanish voluntarily, embarking on a new life together somewhere else in the United States. This theory was fueled by the complete lack of clues about their whereabouts and the reasons for their sudden disappearance. However, this notion conflicts with the deep bonds they both shared with their families and the relatively short duration of their relationship, leading many to doubt the likelihood of a planned disappearance. Further casting doubt on this theory is the complete lack of activity on their social media accounts, cellphones, and bank accounts, which typically might indicate ongoing life activities.

A second, more ominous theory involves the man rumored to have been involved with Audrey. Speculations arose that he might have been a jilted lover seeking revenge, possibly leading him to torch his own car to destroy potential evidence that could link him to Audrey and Jonathan's disappearance. However, the police have been reticent about this man, revealing little regarding the search warrant executed at his residence or his status in the investigation. He has not been publicly named as a suspect, leaving this theory shrouded in uncertainty.

The third theory posits that foul play could be at play. Some speculate that the photo sent from Audrey's cellphone might have been dispatched by someone else, a deliberate act to mislead her sister, investigators, and her family into believing Audrey and Jonathan were together when they were not. This theory raises questions about who might have had access to Audrey's phone and their motives. Additionally, there is a lingering question about whether either Audrey or Jonathan actually traveled to Brawley on May 10, 2017. Another angle of this theory suggests a possible drug deal gone wrong, though this is less substantiated as there have been no reports or indications of the couple being involved in illicit drug activities.

In the aftermath of their disappearance, the families and communities affected by this tragedy have rallied in various ways to keep the hope alive. Prayer vigils have been organized, serving as poignant reminders of the ongoing search and a testament to the communities' solidarity.

Jonathan's mother, grappling with the agony of the unknown, took to Facebook to write letters to her son, clinging to the hope that he might one day respond. Her poignant messages, however, have yet to receive a reply.

A Facebook page dedicated to the couple was established by their loved ones, in a concerted effort to disseminate information and gather leads. This platform has become a digital beacon for those holding onto the hope of finding Audrey and Jonathan.

Throughout this harrowing journey, both families have maintained a close connection, supporting each other through the tumultuous waves of uncertainty and grief. Their united front in the face of such adversity speaks volumes of their resilience and unwavering commitment to finding answers in a case that continues to baffle and sadden all who hear of it.

Heather Teague

Born on a warm spring day, April 25, 1972, Heather Teague's life began in the charming small-town ambiance of Henderson County, Kentucky, nestled just south of the bustling city of Evansville, Indiana. Heather's childhood and teenage years were woven into the fabric of this community, where her vibrant personality and intelligence shone brightly.

Described as a stellar student, Heather was the kind of person who could light up a room with her outgoing and friendly demeanor. Her high school years were a whirlwind of activities; she was a cheerleader, a beloved friend, and a dreamer. With her eyes set on the future, Heather harbored ambitions that ranged from the noble pursuit of becoming a physician or a nurse to the grand aspirations of entering the political arena.

As she tossed her graduation cap into the air, Western Kentucky University beckoned, promising new adventures and learning. However, life, as it often does, took an unexpected turn. Heather's journey through college was cut short, not by lack of intellect or ambition, but by the tendrils of substance use that slowly entangled her life. With a heavy heart, she returned home, finding herself clocking in at a local factory, a stark contrast to the dreams she once held.

The monotonous days at the factory weighed heavily on Heather. The longing to return to college, to reignite the spark of her dreams, never left her. Yet, the shackles of substance use held her back, dragging her further away from the life she envisioned. Her life, once full of potential and hope, seemed to be spiraling out of control.

The summer of 1995 marked a tumultuous chapter in Heather's life. Her existence became nomadic, moving from house to house, her belongings confined to her vehicle. In early August, alarm bells rang as Heather was reported missing. The police, upon finding her, were met with her assurances that she was just 'running around.' But the undercurrents of her life hinted at a deeper unrest.

As August 26, 1995, dawned, 23-year-old Heather found solace in the serene setting of Newburg Beach in Spotsville, Kentucky. This hidden gem, lying right across the Ohio River from Newburgh, Indiana, was a retreat for many, particularly those from Indiana seeking the beach's tranquility.

There, on that fateful day, Heather lay sunbathing, perhaps seeking a moment of peace, oblivious to the eyes that watched her from across the river. In Newburgh, Indiana, a man named Tim, with a telescope in hand, gazed out from his window. Officially, he was bird-watching, but the telescope's lens found Heather instead. Whether by chance or design, his attention was fixed on her, not the birds that might have been soaring in the sky.

Around 12:45 PM, Tim's casual observation took a sinister turn. He noticed a man emerging from the woods, not far from where Heather lay. The man's appearance was odd, to say the least – donning a wig, a mosquito net, jeans, and notably, no shirt.

The stranger casually placed his arm on Heather's back, leaning in as if to say something. Alarmingly, Tim noticed what seemed like a pistol in the man's hand.

The situation escalated quickly. With a sudden, violent motion, the man grabbed Heather by her hair and dragged her towards the woods. In a desperate attempt to maintain her dignity, Heather clutched a towel, trying to cover herself as she was pulled away. Panic-stricken, Tim reached for his phone and dialed 9-1-1. However, a twist of fate intervened – the call connected him to emergency services in Indiana, not Kentucky, where the abduction was unfolding.

Realizing the urgency, Tim made a second call, this time to the Kentucky State Police. The police, upon arriving at the scene, found haunting remnants of the incident: Heather's lounge chair, the top part of her bathing suit near the beach, and deeper in the woods, the bottom part along with the towel she had grabbed. Her vehicle was discovered nearby, adding to the ominous nature of the scene. Yet, Heather was nowhere to be found.

At the same time as Heather's abduction, a man was filming on the Kentucky side of the river, close to where the incident occurred. He had been hired by a local farmer, frustrated by people damaging his crops while driving through his fields. His task was to document the damage and any vehicles present. Among the footage, he inadvertently captured Heather's vehicle, with a tarp laid beside it, its doors wide open.

The camera also picked up a red and white Ford Bronco, distinct with its chrome luggage rack, heading towards the beach. The driver, though blurred in the video, appeared to be a man. Tim, who had been observing through his telescope – allegedly for bird-watching – collaborated with the police to create a sketch of the kidnapper. He described the man as around six feet tall, just over 200 pounds, with a bushy brown beard.

The police launched a hunt for the kidnapper and the distinctive Ford Bronco, appealing to the public for assistance. The owner of the Bronco never came forward, which the police found highly suspicious. Why wouldn't he? Could he be involved in the crime?

Meanwhile, another witness reported seeing a woman struggling with a man in a red Chevette – a car distinctly different from a Ford Bronco. This conflicting account added another layer of complexity to the investigation.

The breakthrough came with a tip about a 30-year-old man named Marvin Ray Dill, who owned a red and white Ford Bronco matching the description, complete with a chrome luggage rack. Marvin's mugshot, taken from a previous arrest, bore a striking resemblance to the man Tim had described. Known to law enforcement, Marvin had a history of bizarre behavior, including a conviction for harassment.

In February 1995, several months before Heather Teague's disappearance, Marvin Ray Dill found himself in a precarious situation. Pulled over by the police in Evansville, Indiana, for approaching young girls from his Ford Bronco, Marvin's vehicle revealed a troubling inventory: marijuana, two guns, two knives, duct tape, rubber gloves, and rope. This alarming discovery led to his arrest on charges related to substances and firearms.

The investigation into Heather's disappearance eventually led the police to Marvin's trailer. However, Marvin was nowhere to be found, and they were met by his wife instead. During their conversation, Marvin's wife cast doubts on her husband's involvement, pointing out that his hair was shorter than what the witness, Tim, had described. This discrepancy suggested that Marvin might not be the person the police were looking for.

The plot thickened when the police received a call from an attorney, claiming to represent Marvin's wife. The attorney expressed concern for Marvin's safety and relayed alarming information from Marvin's wife. She recounted how Marvin had arrived home agitated, instructing her to leave the trailer. She also revealed that Marvin had concealed the Ford Bronco in the woods behind their trailer.

Armed with this new information, the police obtained a search warrant for

Marvin's trailer. On September 1, 1995, in the early hours of the morning, they approached the trailer to execute the warrant. In a tragic turn of events, Marvin ended his life with a firearm as the police closed in, leaving many questions unanswered.

Inside the hidden Ford Bronco, the police discovered blood on the tailgate and hair similar to Heather's, though these findings were never definitively linked to her case. Despite the evidence pointing towards Marvin, there were doubts about whether he acted alone in what was now being treated as a homicide.

The investigation took another twist with the emergence of a second potential suspect: Christopher John Below, a truck driver. Christopher was not only a suspect in another woman's disappearance in 1991, who bore a resemblance to Heather, but he also had a history of violence and highly sexually motivated behavior. He eventually pleaded guilty to attempted involuntary manslaughter in the 1991 case and received a prison sentence of 11 to 18 years.

Moreover, Christopher was suspected in several other disappearances of young women. His presence in the area at the time of Heather's disappearance and his hasty departure from the state afterward raised suspicions. There were unconfirmed rumors that he might have known Marvin, adding another layer of complexity to the case.

Delving into the perplexing case of Heather Teague, a myriad of theories swirl around her tragic disappearance, each one attempting to piece together the fragmented puzzle of what really happened. The evidence, while substantial in some areas, leaves room for speculation and varying interpretations. Let's explore the major theories and scrutinize the evidence supporting and contesting them.

We begin with the theory that Marvin Dill was solely responsible for Heather's murder. The evidence pointing toward this theory is compelling. Marvin Dill, a man with a criminal history of harassing women, possessed items in his vehicle that could be described as tools for abduction, including duct tape, knives, and rope. His vehicle, a red and white Ford Bronco with a distinctive chrome luggage rack, was seen near the kidnapping site. Furthermore, Tim, the man who observed the abduction through his telescope, believed the perpetrator resembled Marvin.

However, the theory becomes tangled when considering the possibility of Marvin collaborating with Christopher, another suspect. It seems illogical for Marvin to have another individual drive his vehicle while he committed the abduction. Marvin's erratic behavior following the police's inquiries, culminating in his suicide, suggests a man desperate to evade confrontation with law enforcement. Notably, Marvin's criminal history indicates he typically acted alone, not in collusion with others.

Turning our attention to the evidence that challenges this theory, Christopher emerges as a credible suspect. His physical description matched the witness's account, much like Marvin. Complicating matters, Marvin's wife questioned whether the man observed by Tim could have been her husband, citing his hair length at the time of the abduction. The perpetrator's use of a wig further obscures the identity, broadening the pool of potential suspects.

Given these factors, when analyzing the evidence, it seems more plausible that Marvin was the lone perpetrator of Heather's murder. His known history, the circumstantial evidence linking him to the scene, and his subsequent actions paint a picture of a man capable of acting alone in such a heinous crime. Yet, the shadow of doubt cast by the involvement of the wig, the potential role of Christopher, and the intricacies of human behavior leave a sliver of uncertainty in this tragic and complex case.

Beyond the theories centering around Marvin and Christopher, there are other, more far-fetched hypotheses that warrant exploration.

One such theory suggests that Heather fell victim to organized crime. However, the evidence supporting this claim is thin at best. While Heather may have dabbled in drugs and led a somewhat erratic lifestyle, these factors alone don't convincingly place her in the crosshairs of a crime syndicate. Moreover, the method of her abduction – being dragged into the woods – seems inconsistent with the more direct approach typically associated with gang-related killings.

Another hypothesis posits that Heather orchestrated her own disappearance to start anew. This theory, while creative, borders on the fantastical. It implies that Heather somehow anticipated that an observer, like Tim with his telescope, would be watching her from across the river, and that she had an accomplice pretend to kidnap her. The idea that Heather, living out of her car, would go to such lengths for a fresh start, complete with a staged abduction, is almost too intricate and convoluted to be feasible. Despite its effectiveness in convincing people of her demise, this theory overlooks the simpler option of just walking away from her current life.

Turning to what might have actually transpired, I propose a theory based on the available evidence and the behavior of the known suspects. Marvin Dill, a criminal with a history of antisocial behavior and offenses against women, could have been scouring Newburgh Beach for potential victims. Upon noticing Heather's vehicle, Marvin might have initially contemplated theft but then decided on abduction upon seeing Heather alone on the beach.

Concerned about being observed, perhaps even considering the likelihood of someone like Tim watching the area, Marvin could have donned a disguise before abducting Heather. In the secluded areas of Kentucky, he might have committed heinous acts before ultimately killing Heather and hiding her body in a location that remains undiscovered.

The capture of Marvin's vehicle on video near the crime scene, an unlikely occurrence in 1995, especially in a remote area, might have signaled to

Marvin that his crime wouldn't go unnoticed. Faced with the prospect of law enforcement closing in and a return to prison, Marvin chose to end his life, thereby foreclosing any chance of a judicial resolution.

This interpretation of the events as a crime of opportunity aligns with the evidence and Marvin's known characteristics. It underscores the unpredictability and brutality of the crime – an unsuspecting woman enjoying a day at the beach, unaware of the danger lurking in the nearby woods.

The closure of the case with Marvin's suicide left many feeling unsatisfied. Friends, family, and law enforcement sought traditional justice through the legal system, a resolution that was denied by Marvin's final act. In the absence of such closure, alternative theories, however unlikely, continue to circulate, perhaps fueled by the discomfort of a criminal dictating the end of the investigation on his own terms. While there's no substantial evidence supporting these alternate theories, the haunting question of "what if" lingers, adding to the tragedy and mystery of Heather Teague's disappearance.

Michael McClain

ichael "Mike" McClain, a spirited 29-year-old from Manchester, New Hampshire, mysteriously disappeared on the night of April 21, 2019. Known for his jovial nature and zest for life, Mike was a beloved figure among his friends and family. His father fondly recalls him as a jokester who embraced life with open arms. Born and raised in the charming town of Stamford, Connecticut, Mike's journey led him to Hester College, now known as Mount Washington College, where he earned a bachelor's degree in Criminal Justice. His passion for helping others shone through in his work with children with autism at Easter Seals, a non-profit organization where he dedicated his time and energy.

On that fateful night, Mike decided to unwind with a few friends at the Tropical Lounge Light Club, now rebranded as the Opus Lounge, located in Nashua, New Hampshire. The evening took an unexpected turn around 1:30 a.m., when a heated altercation erupted between two young women at the nightclub. The dispute, which started inside, quickly spilled onto the streets outside. According to initial reports, Mike, who was acquainted with one of the women, seemed to have intervened in an attempt to defuse the situation. However, it was later confirmed that he played no part in the altercation and did not attempt to break up the fight.

As the situation escalated, the Nashua Police were called to the scene. Upon their arrival, they worked to disperse the crowd and restore order, advising everyone to head home. In the ensuing chaos, Mike's friends lost sight of him. They tried reaching out to him via text around 2:00 a.m., but to no avail. Assuming he had made his way home safely, they departed. However, concern grew when Mike failed to return calls from his mother and grandmother on Easter Sunday, April 21st. The alarm was raised when he didn't show up for family celebrations, a stark deviation from his usual routine.

The following day, April 22, 2019, Mike's roommate, filled with worry and uncertainty, reported him missing after realizing that he hadn't returned home. This marked the beginning of a heart-wrenching journey for Mike's family and friends, as they grappled with his inexplicable disappearance and the profound sense of loss it brought.

Ever since the night of April 20th, when Michael McClain vanished, his loved ones have been engulfed in a whirlwind of sleepless nights and relentless worry. Michael, who had made Manchester his home for several years, was a dedicated worker at Easter Seals. His mysterious disappearance following a night out at the Tropical Lounge in Nashua has left his family and friends grappling with unanswered questions and a deep sense of foreboding.

Edward, Michael's father, remains adamant that his son would never just vanish without a trace, especially without informing his mother of his whereabouts. Mike, as he was affectionately known, had so much to live for, so much potential yet to be realized. The thought of him just disappearing into thin air is inconceivable, uncharacteristic of the Michael they knew and loved. In an effort to find answers, hundreds of missing person posters have been distributed around Nashua and Manchester, each one a silent plea for any information that might shed light on his whereabouts.

The puzzle of that fateful night deepens with every new detail that emerges. Investigative efforts have unearthed footage showing Michael walking along West Hollis Street before abruptly turning into Elder Street, a narrow alleyway. What followed next only adds to the mystery. According to Edward McClain, Michael's father, there was a perplexing phone call made to his boss just before 2:00 a.m. Michael's words were chilling: "They're after me, more than one." The call ended abruptly, and subsequent attempts to reach him went unanswered.

Adding to the enigma were three cryptic text messages sent to his neighbor. The first read, "help lol hour," followed by "we stood aloof," and finally, "Eldridge broke." The ambiguity of these messages has led Michael's parents to speculate that they might have been the result of voice-to-text errors. Nonetheless, their cryptic nature has left everyone baffled.

Further deepening the mystery, Michael's phone was last pinged at a McDonald's on East Hollis Street around 2:00 a.m. on April 21st. This last known location offers a glimmer of hope in tracing his steps, but also raises more questions than answers. What happened to Michael after he got separated from his friends that night? And what did he mean by those enigmatic messages and the ominous phone call to his boss?

Michael, last captured by video surveillance near the Riverfront Landing apartment complex at 11 Bancroft Street, was seen exiting a parking garage at the rear of the complex at about 3:23 a.m., before disappearing from view. This was the last confirmed sighting of Michael, setting the stage for a mystery that continues to baffle all involved.

His parents, driven by a relentless quest for answers, believe that after his visit to McDonald's, Michael stopped at a gas station, possibly in an attempt to make a phone call. Then, for reasons unknown, he proceeded to the aforementioned apartment complex. The motives behind these movements remain as elusive as Michael himself.

It's worth noting that much of the information available seems to emanate from Michael's parents. They have expressed a feeling of bearing the brunt of the investigative efforts, overshadowing what they perceive as limited engagement from the Nashua Police Department. Despite the department's ongoing investigation, Michael's father has voiced frustration over the sporadic updates, which he receives only upon request. This sense of a one-sided effort has only intensified the family's determination to uncover the truth.

Michael's aunt has made a heartfelt appeal to those who were with him on that fateful night, imploring them to come forward with any information, no matter how insignificant it may seem. "You were with him, you have to know something," she pleads, underscoring the impossibility of knowing nothing in a situation so dire.

The family's desire for answers is palpable – they need to know whether they will be welcoming Michael back or preparing for a more solemn farewell. Their resolve is unyielding: they will not rest until Michael is found.

The Nashua Police Department maintains that this remains an open and active investigation. Meanwhile, the description of Michael McClain is circulated widely: a black male, about 5 foot 10 inches tall, with a medium build weighing between 180 to 190 pounds. Distinctive features include a small goatee, short braids, green contact lenses, piercings in both ears, and multiple tattoos on his forearms and hands. On the night he went missing, Michael did not drive to Nashua, adding another layer of mystery to his disappearance.

Laureen Rahn

aureen Ann Rahn's journey through life began on a spring day, April 3, 1966, a day that marked the beginning of a story filled with intrigue and unanswered questions. Born to her mother, Judith, Laureen's early years are shrouded in mystery, a tapestry with more missing threads than those present. The details of her childhood are sparse, a puzzle with crucial pieces missing, leaving us to wonder about the fabric of her early life.

The identity of Laureen's biological father remains an enigma, a shadowy figure absent from the narrative of her life. Rumors and whispers hint at the existence of a sister, yet like so much of Laureen's story, these are mere echoes without substance, details that remain just beyond reach. What we do know, however, paints a picture of a young girl cherished by her mother. The brown-haired, blue-eyed Laureen was the apple of Judith's eye, the center of her universe.

Their world was a modest apartment nestled in the heart of Manchester, New Hampshire. This city, a bustling hub in southern New Hampshire, stands proudly as the most populous city in northern New England. With over 100,000 residents, Manchester is a melting pot of cultures and stories, including Laureen's. The city forms an integral part of the tri-state area, comprising New Hampshire, Maine, and Vermont, and is cradled by the flowing waters of the Merrimack River.

In their third-floor apartment on Merrimack Street, Laureen blossomed into a kind-hearted and dream-filled young girl. Her imagination was a vivid tapestry of dreams and aspirations. She was drawn to the performing arts, with a voice for singing, a passion for dancing, and a heart yearning for the bright lights of Hollywood. Academically, she shone like a star, her intellect a beacon guiding her through school without much trouble.

The bond between Laureen and Judith was a strong one, forged in the fires of single parenthood and mutual reliance. Judith's heart, while open to the possibilities of love, always had Laureen at its center. Men may have come and gone in Judith's life, but Laureen was the unwavering constant, the north star in her mother's sky.

As Laureen entered her teenage years at Parkside Junior High School, she continued to excel academically, though the winds of adolescent rebellion began to whisper through her life. It was nothing drastic – Laureen was far from a rebel – but the usual teenage explorations and minor missteps were part of her journey. Intriguingly, an online post by a former schoolmate hinted at a sudden and mysterious school change. Laureen had spoken of moving to Florida, yet, as it turned out, she had simply transferred to Southside Junior High, a move that wasn't as drastic as it might have seemed.

Amidst these typical teenage explorations, Laureen occasionally dabbled in activities not quite suited for her age. Rumors swirled around a local corner store and its propensity to sell alcohol to minors, a not-so-rare occurrence in the era. Though the legal drinking age was 18 at the time, selling alcohol to a 14-year-old was still a transgression. It's not clear how much Laureen partook in these activities or if Judith was ever aware, but it was a facet of her life that, while not defining, was certainly a part of the tapestry of her adolescence.

The story of Judith and her daughter, Laureen, took an unexpected turn with the arrival of a new man in Judith's life. He was a tennis enthusiast, rumored in many papers to have played professionally, though he never quite reached a level that would etch his name into the annals of the sport. His identity remains a mystery, as it was never publicly disclosed. Judith and her boyfriend would often travel to various tennis tournaments, with Laureen always in tow. These trips were a welcome escape for them, a chance to bond over the excitement of the game and enjoy time together as a family.

However, on April 20, 1980, a day that would later be etched in their memories, Judith was preparing for yet another tournament. This time, Laureen, embracing the spirit of independence typical of a teenager on the cusp of spring break, requested to stay home alone. Judith, though initially reluctant, eventually consented, planning to return late that night. Laureen was overjoyed, grateful for this newfound freedom.

Manchester basked in the warmth of a 75-degree day, a typical prelude to a spring break in New England, but as evening approached, the temperature dipped to a chilly 37 degrees, a stark reminder of the region's unpredictable weather. Before leaving, Judith reminded Laureen to lock up and go to bed early, expressing her love and expectations for good behavior. Little did she know, this routine farewell would be the last exchange she would have with her daughter.

That evening, according to a friend of Laureen's who was at the apartment, was meant to be a simple gathering. Laureen had invited her and a male friend over for a casual hangout – some drinks, television, and laughter. They were cautious, unsure of when Judith would return, but confident they would wrap up their little get-together in time. Contrary to some rumors, Laureen's friend denied the presence of another male guest that night.

Judith, reflecting on that night years later, expressed doubts about the completeness of the story presented to the authorities. She believed there were details left untold. She returned home between midnight and 1:30 a.m., entering a building shrouded in darkness. The usually lit hallways were eerily dim, a situation that unsettled her. She considered the possibility of a power outage but found it odd that the entire building was affected.

Upon reaching her apartment, Judith discovered the front door unlocked, a departure from the instructions she had left for Laureen. Inside, everything appeared normal, but a check of the back door revealed it slightly ajar, adding to the night's peculiarities. After securing the door, Judith headed to Laureen's bedroom.

Here, the story becomes muddled with conflicting timelines and reports. According to multiple sources, Judith opened Laureen's bedroom door and saw her daughter seemingly asleep. Quietly, she closed the door, deciding to address the unlocked doors in the morning.

As Judith entered her living room on that fateful night, she noticed subtle signs of something amiss – a blanket and pillow on the couch, suggesting that Laureen might have been there earlier. Another odd detail caught her eye: a pair of brand-new shoes, recently acquired by Laureen, lay abandoned in a corner. This was uncharacteristic of her daughter, who was usually meticulous about her belongings.

The case of Laureen's disappearance is mired in conflicting narratives and discrepancies, especially regarding the events of that night. According to the Charlie Project's account, Judith retired to her bedroom, unaware of the unfolding mystery. It wasn't until the next morning, upon entering Laureen's bedroom, that she discovered a startling truth. The person she thought was Laureen asleep in her bed was actually Laureen's friend who had stayed over. This revelation raised immediate alarm about Laureen's whereabouts.

However, this version of events contradicts official police reports. Another theory suggests that Judith, perhaps driven by a mother's intuition, re-entered Laureen's room later that night with the intention of waking her daughter. It was then that she discovered the friend in Laureen's bed and realized Laureen was missing. Coupled with the darkened hallways, this discovery painted a chilling picture.

The police were called at approximately 3:45 a.m. Judith, distraught, explained the evening's events to the responding officers. Initially, the police considered the possibility that Laureen had run away, a theory that seemed plausible given the circumstances. Laureen's friend recounted a night of innocent teenage fun – drinking wine, laughing, and eventually falling asleep. However, the friend's narrative left many questions unanswered, and the theory of a runaway began to lose ground.

During the initial investigation, a disturbing discovery was made. The apartment's electricity was functioning correctly; someone had deliberately unscrewed the light bulbs in the hallways of each floor. This sinister detail suggested a more nefarious scenario than a simple runaway case.

The police interviewed the male friend who had been at the apartment that night. He was never considered a person of interest, and his account matched that of Laureen's female friend. He recalled sneaking out the back door to avoid being caught drinking with minors and specifically remembered hearing Laureen lock the door behind him. This detail conflicted with Judith's discovery of the back door being unlocked and slightly open upon her return.

Little is known about this male friend, but it's speculated he was older than Laureen and possibly provided the alcohol. Despite this, authorities did not believe he was involved in Laureen's disappearance. Initially convinced Laureen had run away, the police began to doubt this theory as more details emerged. The tampering with the light bulbs seemed too calculated to be a coincidence, and there was no evidence to support the runaway hypothesis. Laureen had left everything behind – her purse, clothes, even her wallet.

As time passed with no sightings or leads, frustration mounted among the investigators. The runaway theory lost traction, and the police began to consider other possibilities.

As the mystery of Loreen Rahn's disappearance deepened, investigators formed a theory that on the night of her vanishing, she might have left the apartment and encountered danger outside. The absence of any signs of struggle or disturbance within the apartment supported this idea. Despite thorough investigations, the lack of concrete evidence made it challenging to move forward with certainty.

The investigation, shrouded in ambiguity, left many questions unanswered. It was unclear if the apartment or the light bulbs, a curious aspect of the case, had been checked for fingerprints. If such measures were taken, they unfortunately led to no significant discoveries. Further interviews with Laureen's friends, who were present that night, revealed no new information. They reported nothing unusual – no unexpected visitors, strange behaviors, or alarming phone calls.

As the days turned into months, the case of Laureen's disappearance gradually receded from the public eye. The once-urgent search seemed to fade as rapidly as the 14-year-old had disappeared into the night. The number of officers assigned to the case dwindled, reflecting the lack of progress and leads. In Manchester, Laureen's story became a haunting cautionary tale, a reminder of the unpredictability and fragility of life.

However, a bizarre twist emerged six months after Laureen's disappearance. Judith discovered unusual charges on her phone bill – three calls made from a hotel in Santa Monica, California, around three months after Laureen vanished. In the era before cell phones, these calls indicated that someone knew Judith's phone number and had used it to charge the calls. This strange occurrence led Judith to wonder if Laureen might have made these calls. But there was no clear connection to California; neither Judith nor Laureen had known anyone on the West Coast.

Investigations into these calls revealed that two were made to a hotel in Santa Ana, California, but led nowhere. The third call, however, was to a teen sexual assistance hotline, which traced back to a physician in California. When questioned initially, the doctor denied any knowledge of Laureen or the hotline. This aspect of the investigation seemed to reach a dead end.

Adding to the eerie nature of the case, Judith and her sister received numerous anonymous calls over the following years, often around 3:45 a.m., the same time Judith had called the police to report Laureen missing. These calls were silent, contributing to the haunting atmosphere surrounding Laureen's disappearance. The frequency of these calls increased during Christmas, leading Judith to change her phone number eventually.

A year after Laureen's disappearance, a family member believed she spotted a young woman resembling Laureen in Boston, Massachusetts. However, this sighting was never confirmed, and the woman in question vanished before any interaction could occur.

The case stagnated for years, with few leads and no significant developments. It was not until five years later, in 1985, that two noteworthy incidents occurred. Firstly, the young man who had been in Laureen's apartment the night she vanished tragically took his own life. The lack of public information about him makes it difficult to ascertain any connection to Laureen's disappearance.

The second incident in 1985 involved the doctor connected to the teen sexual assistance hotline. This time, he was more forthcoming, revealing that it was not uncommon for young runaway girls to visit his wife. He even mentioned that one of these girls resembled Laureen and claimed to be from New Hampshire. However, the details about this hotline and the nature of these visits remained murky and unsettling.

Further adding to the complexity of the case, the doctor mentioned Annie Sprinkle, born Ellen Steinberg, a well-known adult film star at the time, as someone who might have information about Laureen. Steinberg was a friend of the doctor's wife, but the context of her potential knowledge about Laureen was never clarified.

Another lead emerged when law enforcement reached out to Annie Sprinkle, a prominent figure in the adult film industry during the 70s and 80s. Despite her past career, Sprinkle, who had transitioned to a role as a sex educator and later earned academic degrees in human sexuality, vehemently denied having any knowledge of Loreen or any involvement with runaways. The police, unable to find any connection between Steinberg and the case, hit yet another dead end.

Steinberg's life after her film career was marked by significant achievements and a stable personal life, including her marriage to Beth Stevens in 2007. It's notable that throughout the decades since Loreen vanished, Steinberg has maintained a clean legal record. The investigation did include a review of Steinberg's films to see if Loreen could be identified, but this effort turned up nothing.

Five years after Loreen's disappearance, the case saw a couple of bizarre developments: the suicide of a former friend of Loreen and the strange allegations linking a doctor to the adult film star. These leads, however perplexing, failed to shed light on the mystery of Loreen's whereabouts.

In 1986, driven by a mother's relentless pursuit of truth, Judith hired a private investigator to delve into the mysterious phone calls charged to her account back in 1980. The investigator uncovered that the hotel from which the calls were made was reportedly linked to a child pornography ring led by an individual known as Dr. Z. This unsettling coincidence – a connection to a doctor running a teen sexual assistance hotline and calls from a location tied to child pornography – raised more questions than answers. However, no concrete link was established between Dr. Z, the other doctor, or Loreen.

In a bizarre twist later that year, Roger Mareias, a childhood friend of Loreen's, received a cryptic phone call while he was away, leaving his mother to answer. The female caller, identifying herself as Laureen or Lori, claimed to be an ex-girlfriend of Roger. The conversation was brief and ended abruptly, leaving no further clues. Judith, convinced that the phone calls made to her in 1980 were from Loreen, speculated if this could have been another attempt by her daughter to reach out.

The last reported sighting of Loreen occurred in 1988 in Anchorage, Alaska. A witness, struck by the resemblance of a local sex worker to Loreen, as seen on a missing-persons flyer, contacted the authorities. Despite their efforts, the police were unable to locate this woman, leaving the sighting unconfirmed. The possibility that it was Loreen remains a matter of speculation, with no substantial evidence to verify the claim.

In the years following the last reported sighting of Loreen Rahn, her story tragically faded into a somber silence. No further clues or sightings emerged, leaving her family and investigators in a state of painful uncertainty. Judith, Loreen's mother, remarried and eventually moved to Florida, but she never lost hope that her daughter might still be out there. In her relentless quest for answers, Judith even turned to psychics in recent years, hoping to uncover any clue about her daughter's whereabouts.

Judith has consistently maintained her belief that the three mysterious calls made in 1980 were indeed from Loreen. She also suspects that one of Loreen's childhood friends knows more than she has shared with the authorities. This lingering suspicion adds another layer of complexity and frustration to an already heartbreaking case.

In an effort to find new leads, authorities and researchers began re-examining other disappearances in the area that bore similarities to Loreen's case. The first case considered was that of 15-year-old Rachel Elizabeth Garden, who vanished from Newton, New Hampshire, just a month before Loreen. Like Loreen, Garden was initially thought to be a runaway, but a witness later reported seeing her talking to men in a car on the night she disappeared. Despite a confession from one of these men, her remains were never found, and her case remains unsolved.

Another hauntingly similar case is that of 15-year-old Shirley Ann McBride from Manchester. Frustrated with her parents' strict rules, McBride moved to Concord to live with her sister. In July 1984, she left her sister's apartment to visit her boyfriend and was never seen again. Initially labeled a runaway, authorities later theorized she met with foul play. Her parents had her declared legally dead in 1996, but her fate remains unknown.

The disappearance of Denise Denault, a 25-year-old mother of two, also bears a striking resemblance to Loreen's case. Denault lived just two blocks from Loreen's apartment and vanished in June 1980 after leaving a social gathering. Despite the proximity and timing of their disappearances, no concrete connection between Loreen and Denault has been established. Both women's physical resemblance has been noted, but it hasn't led to any solid leads.

In 2017, 37 years after Denault's disappearance, a joint effort by the FBI and the Manchester Police led to a search in a wooded area behind public housing on Kimball Street. The specifics behind the decision to search this area were not disclosed, but the use of heavy equipment indicated a significant effort. Unfortunately, this search, like many others, failed to bring closure to the mysteries surrounding these tragic disappearances.

The intensive search for clues in Denise Denault's disappearance spanned several days but ultimately yielded no new discoveries. In subsequent discussions with the media, police highlighted a potentially significant detail: Denault had lived just two doors down from a man known as Bob Evans. More infamously, Evans is also identified as Terry Peder Rasmussen, the prime suspect in the Bear Brook State Park murders in Allenstown, New Hampshire, just 20 miles north of Manchester.

The proximity of these cases – three young women disappearing within a 30-mile radius and a four-year period – raises the chilling possibility that they might be connected to Rasmussen, a known serial predator. While some see a potential link between Loreen Rahn's abduction and Rasmussen's crimes, others view it as mere coincidence, citing the lack of concrete evidence tying these cases together.

Loreen Rahn's disappearance remains a deeply troubling and enigmatic case. Despite being officially open, it has languished in the realm of cold cases, with no new information or leads for years. For Judith, the pain of losing her daughter remains as acute as it was in 1980.

In the absence of solid evidence, two main theories have been proposed. The first theory posits that Loreen may have been abducted and forced into sex work, potentially linked to child pornography rings, as suggested by the mysterious calls from California and the connections to Dr. Z's alleged pornography ring and the teen sexual assistance hotline. The second theory suggests that Loreen might have been quickly murdered after her abduction, possibly by a predator who used the darkness of the unlit hallways in her building to his advantage.

Loreen Rahn, at the time of her disappearance, was a Caucasian female with brown hair and blue eyes, standing 5 feet 4 inches tall and weighing approximately 90 pounds. She was last seen wearing a white V-neck sweater, a blue plaid blouse, jeans, brown shoes, a heart-shaped gold ring, and a silver and blue necklace, and she had a prominent scar on her upper leg. If alive today, Loreen would be 53 years old.

Age-progressed photographs have been created to depict what Loreen might look like now, 39 years after her disappearance. For Judith, each passing year adds to the agonizing uncertainty of her daughter's fate. Despite consulting psychics and clinging to the hope of potential leads, no concrete evidence has emerged to shed light on what happened to Loreen.

The heartbreaking reality for Judith is living with the unknown – what life might Loreen have built for herself? Could she have been a mother, an actress? Judith holds onto the belief that her daughter was alive for some time after her disappearance and dreams of the day she might see her face again. For nearly four decades, the truth about Loreen Rahn's fate has remained shrouded in mystery, but the hope endures that someday, light will be shed on this enduring and tragic enigma.

Nefertiri Trader

Nefertiri Trader, born on February 21st, 1981, in Delaware, was affectionately nicknamed Nephi by her friends and family. As a mother of three and the eldest sibling, Nephi was well-regarded in her community. In this case analysis, I will use both Nefertiti's formal name and her nickname. Her cousin William Trader described her as an outgoing and enjoyable person, saying, "She is real fun to be around and if you don't like her, you will love to not like her. She's a real good person." Her mother, Denise, and others close to her, echoed this sentiment, highlighting her outgoing nature and popularity in her community.

Professionally, Nephi worked at Christiana Hospital in Newark, Delaware, as a housekeeper, aspiring to advance to a Patient Transport role. She resided in the Saddle Brook subdivision on Freedom Trail in Newcastle, Delaware. Nephi maintained a strong bond with her mother, Denise, with whom she spoke daily. At one point, Denise even lived with Nephi for a few years.

Before her abduction, Nephi was on medical leave from Christiana Hospital due to an unspecified medical procedure. On the evening of June 29, 2014, the situation appeared normal. Nephi drove her cousin William Trader, who was temporarily living with her and her children, to work. Later, she discussed the BET Awards over the phone with her mother, a typical activity for them. That night, Nephi was at home with her 17-year-old son and younger daughter; the whereabouts of her third child remain unknown.

From this point, the account of events is based on a witness's perspective and not established facts. On the early morning of June 30, 2014, around 3:30 a.m., Nefertiti Trader visited a local 7-Eleven store at 273 Airport Road, a short drive from her Saddlebrook home. After purchasing items, she returned home, exited her silver 2000 Acura RL with Delaware license plate number 404-893, and walked towards her front door, but tragically, she never entered her house. Nefertiti was unexpectedly ambushed and abducted, forcibly taken and placed in the back seat of her car.

Although there was no publicly released surveillance footage of Nefertiti at the 7-Eleven, the Newcastle Police Department confirmed that she did visit the store, wearing a pink sweatsuit, and made a purchase. It remains unverified whether she was driving her vehicle or with someone else. Nefertiti bought a pack of Newport cigarettes, two cups of coffee, and a loaf of bread. The store clerk, familiar with Nefertiti as a regular customer, noted it was unusual for her to visit so early in the morning.

Before delving deeper into her disappearance, it's important to understand the layout of the Saddlebrook community. Saddlebrook, situated off Christiana Road (Route 273), is a one-way-in, one-way-out neighborhood, with no intersecting streets for alternate exits. The subdivision is shaped like a square, with homes on Freedom Trail and an open field in the center. The community consists of duplex-style homes, closely spaced, offering limited privacy. Exiting Saddlebrook requires a right turn onto Christiana Road.

A witness, her neighbor Joe Robinson, reportedly heard noise around 4 AM, prompting him to look out from his upper-level bedroom window. He observed an unknown individual, wearing a black hoodie and tan shorts, dragging Nefertiti and placing her in the backseat of her car. It was unclear whether she was conscious or unconscious, or how exactly she was placed in the vehicle. The witness did not contact the police, assuming the person was taking Nefertiti to the hospital due to illness.

Joe Robinson, Nefertiti Trader's neighbor, claimed that her home was often bustling with activity. Intriguingly, his accounts of the events on that fateful morning have varied over time. This discrepancy will be explored further in my analysis. Additionally, an interview with Joe sheds light on his perspective: he saw someone dragging Nefertiti out of her house and into a car, but assumed she was being taken to the hospital due to illness.

Nefertiti, it appears, never made it inside her home after returning from the 7-Eleven. She managed to get out of her car and was near her front porch when the ambush and abduction took place. William Trader, Nefertiti's 17-year-old son, who was at home, reported hearing a commotion but found no one when he checked. It's assumed he thought the noise was inside the house, not realizing the abduction was happening outside.

The next morning, Denise, Nefertiti's mother, tried to contact her daughter, as was their routine, but Nefertiti's phone was off. Denise initially thought Nefertiti might have returned to work early from medical leave. Concern grew when she couldn't reach Nefertiti later that day.

William Trader, Nefertiti's cousin, arrived at the house to find a loaf of bread on the ground, her shoes and cigarettes on the porch - an unusual scene for Nefertiti. Denise, alarmed, called the police, who took over two hours to respond.

The scene at the house was telling: cigarettes and an unopened condom on the porch, two cups of coffee, and Nefertiti's flip-flops neatly placed at the front door. A smashed loaf of bread, seemingly stepped on, lay on the lawn. It appeared to be a scene of struggle. Nefertiti's car was missing. Denise called her other daughter, and together with the police, they began canvassing the neighborhood.

When they spoke to Joe Robinson, he shared his account of that morning's events. Another neighbor mentioned having a camera, but it wasn't active that night, a missed opportunity to capture the abduction.

A breakthrough came when Nefertiti's car was spotted on surveillance footage from a nearby Verizon store, but the driver's identity remained unknown. After this sighting, neither Nefertiti nor her car were seen again.

Delaware issued a Gold Alert for Nefertiti, used when a senior citizen, a suicidal person, or someone with a disability is missing. It's assumed this was due to her medical leave, though the nature of her medical condition wasn't publicly disclosed.

Robinson's tale takes an intriguing twist as he alleges that drug dealing, specifically cocaine, was a frequent occurrence at Nefertiti's house. However, Denise, Nefertiti's mother, strongly refutes this claim. Having lived with her daughter and grandchildren, Denise asserts that their home in Saddlebrook was free from such illicit activities, and there are no public reports to suggest otherwise.

Robinson's accounts continue to evolve. Initially, he claimed to be awakened by a loud noise, but later, he said he was already awake and drawn to the window by the light on Nefertiti's porch. From his vantage point, he observed her conversing with an unidentified individual before being dragged into her car. These changing stories add a layer of mystery and complexity to the case.

Weeks after Nefertiti's disappearance, rumors surfaced that her phone was briefly powered on then off again. This tantalizing detail hints at the possibility that someone still had her phone, choosing not to discard it despite the growing media attention. This raises questions: Why retain the phone? Could it hold clues to her abduction?

When examining the various theories surrounding Nefertiti's abduction, two main ideas emerge: one suggests she was followed home, possibly from the 7-Eleven, and another posits that she was targeted for sexual assault. The first theory seems less likely, given the lack of evidence that she was followed, and Robinson didn't report seeing any other vehicles near the time of her abduction. If she was indeed followed, it raises questions about the logistics of such an act, especially if it involved more than one person.

The scenario becomes even more puzzling when considering the practicalities of an abduction involving multiple assailants. Why use Nefertiti's car if there was another vehicle involved? And if only one person was seen, how did they arrive at the scene? Were they local, making it easier to execute such a plan on foot?

These unanswered questions make the case increasingly complex. The absence of additional cars or witnesses leaves a gap in understanding the true nature of this abduction. It's a scenario that seems to point towards a single abductor, but without more evidence, the truth remains elusive, shrouded in a veil of mystery and conjecture.

Let's ponder an intriguing possibility - could the abductor have arrived by bus? While it might seem unlikely, there is a bus route, Route 51, running through Delaware 273, from downtown to Christiana Mall, passing near Nefertiti's home. However, this route starts operating at 5:25 a.m., well after the abduction occurred around 4 a.m. This timing discrepancy casts doubt on the bus theory, leaving us to wonder how the abductor reached Nefertiti's home so early in the morning.

Shifting focus to the second theory, a potential sexual assault, we find an unopened condom conspicuously placed on Nefertiti's porch chair alongside her cigarettes. This raises several questions: why was it left there? Could it have been a clue, or perhaps an accident? If the intention was sexual assault, why abduct Nefertiti instead of forcing entry into her home? The close-knit, duplex-style neighborhood would have made it risky for an assailant to attempt such a crime without being noticed.

The method of abduction itself is puzzling. If you were to abduct an adult, would you risk placing them in the backseat, where they could potentially attack you or escape? This leads to the speculation that Nefertiti might have been incapacitated, allowing the abductor to control the situation more easily. Given Nefertiti's petite stature, the abductor likely overpowered her quickly, possibly without attracting much attention.

The key question remains: how did the abductor know Nefertiti would be out at that early hour? The store clerk's statement that Nefertiti frequently visited the 7-Eleven in the evenings doesn't provide a clear answer. Was this a random abduction, or did Nefertiti unknowingly reveal her early morning plans to someone?

Then there's the matter of the two coffees Nefertiti purchased. According to Denise, they were for Nefertiti and her daughter, a routine gesture. But why start the day so unusually early, especially during summer when school is out?

Regarding Nefertiti's children, we know two were home at the time of the abduction. Her son heard noises but found nothing amiss downstairs, likely because the abduction occurred outside. When did the children realize their mother was missing, and did they notice the scene on the porch?

And finally, where is Nefertiti's car? It could hold crucial evidence. Has anyone checked nearby water sources, like the Delaware River? Could the car have been dismantled or hidden?

Each unanswered question adds to the mystery of Nefertiti Trader's disappearance, especially considering the possibility that Robinson's account might not be entirely accurate or truthful. The truth lies in piecing together these disparate clues, each potentially leading us closer to solving this perplexing case.

Asha Kreimer

Born under the Hawaiian sun on May 2, 1989, to Russell and Jeannie, Asha grew up with her older sister Ganji. Their early childhood was marked by a significant move in 1991 to the shores of Redcliffe, Australia, where Asha became a dual citizen of both the United States and Australia.

In the backdrop of their lives, however, lay a tumultuous event: the divorce of their parents in 1996. This led Asha and her family to an adventure into the unknown as her mother, a nurse, accepted a job in a remote Aboriginal community. Described as unsafe by her mother, this town instilled a sense of fear in young Asha, a feeling that was exacerbated when, at the tender age of 12 or 13, she was stopped by a police officer regarding a local violent crime. This encounter left such a deep impact on Asha that her mother, noticing her reluctance to even leave the house, decided to send her to boarding school.

At boarding school, Asha blossomed. She excelled academically and thrived in sports, showcasing her resilience and adaptability. After high school, she reunited with her mother, but the wheels of change were already in motion. In 2011, Asha and Ganji, driven by a sudden impulse, embarked on a new journey to San Francisco, California. There, Asha's life took a romantic turn when she met Jamai Gail. Their love story unfolded rapidly, and they soon found themselves navigating the challenges of life together.

The couple's journey led them to Albion, California, in 2013, where they shared a home filled with the joy of several pets. Asha found employment at a hotel and a dog nursery, and around this time, she began using marijuana. By early September 2015, after a trip to Los Angeles, Asha expressed a desire to transform her life, focusing on improving her relationships and achieving personal goals like obtaining a driver's license. Despite a period of low mood and lost confidence, she remained optimistic about her future, dreaming of marriage and starting a family.

However, anxiety crept in as she anticipated the visit of her Australian friend Sally Scales. Sleepless nights became a new norm for Asha, who was usually a sound sleeper. The tension peaked on September 18, when Asha, Jamai, and Sally were together at her residence. In a startling moment, Asha emerged from her room, revealing the sudden recall of a traumatic experience.

From childhood, Asha believed in the power of photographs to unlock the chambers of memory, a belief that would later play a crucial role in her life. As her mental state became increasingly concerning, Asha and her boyfriend, Jamai, reached a consensus on the need for professional help, planning to seek a therapist the following Monday.

However, the weekend unfolded with a series of alarming events. On Saturday, Asha's behavior took a strange turn; she was unusually quiet, responding to conversation with mere shrugs and peculiar hand gestures. Concerned, Jamai took her to the emergency room in Fort Bragg on Sunday, September 20. But the hospital visit spiraled into chaos. Asha's non-cooperation with the mental health professionals culminated in a dramatic escape attempt, leading to a frenzied situation where it took multiple people to restrain her.

Diagnosed with a manic episode and deemed a danger to herself and others, Asha was committed under California's Code 5150. In a bewildering twist, she falsely confessed to murdering her neighbor Joy Mae Taylor, who was, in fact, alive and well. Despite her unstable condition and self-harm gestures, the clinicians discharged her without any mental health assessment or treatment, leaving her in a vulnerable state.

The journey back to Albion was fraught with peril. Asha's erratic behavior escalated, attempting to jump out of the moving vehicle. That night, she remained restless, fully dressed, and exhibited unusual actions like starting their vehicle without a license and burning paper with a candle.

The next morning, Asha's disappearance from the house sparked a frantic search by Jamai and Sally. They found her near a tree, eerily watching them. Her return home was short-lived; she bolted out again, running barefoot over gravel without showing any signs of pain—a testament to her alarming and perplexing state of mind. In a desperate attempt to calm her, Jamai, Sally, and Asha went for a drive, hoping the motion and change of scenery would bring some tranquility to her troubled mind.

The enigmatic journey of Asha Kreimer took a turn into the unknown at the Rollerville Café in Point Arena, California. In this quaint eatery, Asha's silence spoke volumes - she barely spoke and left her food untouched, wrapped in her own thoughts. A seemingly ordinary moment took a mysterious twist when her friend Sally stepped away to the restroom. Seconds later, Asha followed, trailing silently like a shadow. But Sally never encountered Asha in the restroom; instead, Asha vanished from the restaurant, stepping out into a day that would mark her disappearance.

Three hours later, her boyfriend, alarmed by her absence, called the police. Asha was last seen wearing a gray hoodie and black skinny jeans, with no shoes, no identification, cash, or credit cards. Even her cell phone was left behind, found near their residence. That day, Asha became an enigma, with unconfirmed sightings at a nearby beach and a store, adding layers to the mystery.

The police pieced together a curious detail: Asha had returned home, possibly to fetch her German Shepherd, who was also missing, leaving her other dog behind. This selective decision raised questions - why one dog and not the other? Rumors swirled about Asha possibly living under an alias, suggesting a voluntary disappearance.

Adding to the intrigue, Eddie Ryan, Asha's neighbor and the subject of her false murder confession, himself disappeared three years later. While no apparent connection exists between the two cases, the coincidence adds a peculiar twist to the tale.

Asha's mother, Jeannie, frequently travels from Australia to California, tirelessly searching for her daughter. Despite encountering many who claim to have seen Asha, Jeannie's quest remains unfulfilled.

Delving into the possibility of a mental health condition, evidence suggests that Asha might have been grappling with bipolar disorder. With a family history of schizophrenia and bipolar disorder, and hospital staff observing signs of a manic episode, the pieces of the puzzle begin to align.

She was haunted by inappropriate guilt, convinced she had committed a grave crime against her neighbor. Her sleep was erratic, disrupted for days on end. In the hospital, Asha displayed what was described as superhuman strength and a startling lack of sensitivity to pain. These extraordinary manifestations hint at a deeper, more complex condition.

Beyond bipolar disorder, Asha's symptoms could point to schizoaffective disorder, a formidable fusion of bipolar and schizophrenia characteristics. This diagnosis might explain her catatonic-like symptoms, painting a picture of a mind in turmoil, trapped between reality and delusion.

The most baffling aspect of Asha's story is her premature release from the hospital. Clinicians suspected a manic episode with psychosis, yet she was sent away, untreated. This critical juncture in her mental health journey, possibly her first brush with psychotic symptoms, was met with a disturbingly lax response. The hospital's failure to provide adequate care during this pivotal moment may have sealed her fate.

Asha's case raises crucial questions about mental health care. First-break psychosis is a critical period demanding immediate and intensive care, unlike subsequent episodes where established support systems may exist. Asha's case was a missed opportunity for intervention at a time when everything was uncharted and perilous.

The mystery of Asha Kreimer's disappearance is riddled with theories. One suggests she ran away to start anew, drawing parallels to her impulsive move from Australia to San Francisco. Yet, this theory crumbles under the weight of contradictions: no money, no ID, not even shoes. If she returned home for her German Shepherd, it adds to her burden rather than aiding her escape. Asha's mother speculates that the dog's disappearance might be a mere coincidence, perhaps seizing its own chance to escape amidst the chaos.

Another theory posits that Asha met with foul play after leaving the restaurant, a theory based on the possibility that someone took advantage of her vulnerable state. However, the likelihood of encountering a murderer just outside a café seems statistically improbable. Yet, in Asha's fragile mental state, her own actions may have inadvertently steered her towards danger.

Asha's story remains shrouded in mystery, a labyrinth of theories and possibilities, each more haunting than the last. Her journey through mental turmoil and the subsequent disappearance is a poignant reminder of the complexities of the human mind and the critical importance of timely and effective mental health care.

Jake Latiolais

Jake Latiolais, a 22-year-old man, mysteriously disappeared on August 29, 2014. He was a Caucasian male, standing 5 feet 10 inches tall, weighing around 150 pounds, with brown hair and eyes. A notable feature was a cross-shaped scar on his left wrist. At the time, Jake possibly had a short mustache and beard and was a smoker. Significantly, he had a broken foot, necessitating the use of crutches and an orthopedic boot.

This particular detail about Jake's condition plays a significant role in his story, which will be revisited later. I had a conversation with Tina about Jake's personality. It's vital to acknowledge that the individuals in these stories are real, each with their own set of preferences, quirks, and people who miss them. According to Tina, Jake was inherently quiet, had a passion for fishing, and enjoyed working on cars. He was the kind of person who sought to understand everything in depth. This trait of Jake's was especially evident when, as a teenager, he completely dismantled and rebuilt a car in his mother's garage, a feat few could imagine accomplishing.

Jake's early years were challenging; he was diagnosed with lymphoma at two or three years old, which he eventually overcame. This experience contributed to his resilience throughout life. As an adult, Jake was extraordinarily industrious, holding three jobs, mainly to support his young daughter from a previous relationship. He was in the process of seeking custody of his daughter, having already prepared a living arrangement and a secured loan for a business venture. Interestingly, it was later discovered that Jake was not the biological father of another child he believed was his.

This backdrop makes the subsequent events more perplexing. Jake was responsible and committed to his daughter's well-being. Tina also mentioned that he was known for his cheerful, clownish nature and had no known mental health issues or drug use.

On the early morning of August 29, 2014, the East Baton Rouge Sheriff's Office received two anonymous calls reporting that someone had jumped off the Horace Wilkinson Bridge, a constantly busy interstate crossing the Mississippi River. The first call was nonchalant, while the second, from the same number, had a distinctly different tone, as if the caller was trying to disguise their identity as two separate people.

In one call, the informant claimed to be driving eastbound, while in another, they stated they were headed westbound, an impossible feat given the short time frame. Aside from this anonymous caller, there were no other witnesses to what transpired on the bridge that night. A truck was observed in the crucial right-hand lane leading to West Baton Rouge. Despite the lane's usual congestion and poor lighting on the bridge, the truck, left unscathed, caught no one's attention.

When officers arrived, they found the truck with its engine still running, a phone, and cigarettes inside. Earlier, a state trooper had reported seeing the truck on the bridge, accompanied by a grey car, a detail that was not further investigated.

It turned out that the truck belonged to Jake Latiolais, who has not been seen since that night. The East Baton Rouge Sheriff's Office quickly concluded that Jake had parked on the bridge, jumped off, and committed suicide. However, Tina, Jake's mother, firmly disagrees with this theory. She believes that it wasn't in Jake's nature to take his own life.

Despite the common denial in such cases, Tina's skepticism is backed by several compelling reasons. Significantly, Jake's body has never been found. Although authorities claimed to have searched the river, the effort appeared minimal, and the case was hastily closed as a suicide. No one has surfaced in the eight years since Jake's disappearance.

Investigators labeled the case as a mere missing person's case. However, they never inspected Jake's residence, a trailer he shared with a roommate. When Tina visited, she discovered the trailer in a state of disarray, with signs of violence like a broken window and holes in the walls. Jake's valuable possessions, including his TV, gaming console, and guns, were missing.

Jake's roommate claimed he slept through the night and didn't hear anything unusual. He stated that when he went to bed, the trailer was in its normal state, but when he woke up, it was in disarray. Furthermore, the roommate mentioned he did not see Jake on the 29th.

Complicating matters, Jake's trailer was later destroyed in a fire. According to Tina, there's no official report of the incident. She was informed that the fire started from a nearby truck, leading to the trailer's ignition. This incident meant any potential evidence in Jake's home was irretrievably lost.

Tina has faced considerable challenges in her pursuit of the truth, often feeling dismissed by the police. She spoke to a detective who initially appeared to be involved in the case, even discussing it on Crime Stoppers. However, upon meeting Tina, the detective claimed the case wasn't under his jurisdiction and more information was needed to reopen it.

Jurisdiction issues have further complicated the investigation. The Horace Wilkinson Bridge, where Jake's truck was found, is situated between West Baton Rouge and East Baton Rouge, creating ongoing disputes over jurisdictional responsibility. Initially, the East Baton Rouge authorities took charge, even informing Jake's father about his presumed death. Yet, they later attempted to transfer the case to West Baton Rouge.

Tina made efforts to engage with West Baton Rouge authorities, spending three hours presenting the case details to a detective, only to be dismissed again. These jurisdictional disputes also served as the reason for not searching Jake's trailer.

Tina's last update indicated that West Baton Rouge Police were still denying responsibility, redirecting her back to East Baton Rouge. Consequently, there's uncertainty about who, if anyone, is actively investigating Jake's case.

Despite these challenges and the unclear circumstances surrounding the case, the official stance remains that Jake's disappearance was a suicide, a conclusion that Tina and others continue to question.

There was an important piece of information in Jake's case that had not been shared yet: at the time he went missing, Jake had a broken right foot and a broken thumb. He was reliant on crutches for moving around and was wearing an orthopedic boot, which he was advised to remove only for showering and dressing. This fact significantly influenced the theory of him potentially jumping off the bridge.

Jake's mother, Tina, discovered his orthopedic boot in his bedroom, but his crutches were not found. If Jake had indeed jumped into the river, while it was likely that his body might have sunk, the crutches, being buoyant, would have floated and either been spotted or washed ashore. Their absence from the scene indicated that they either were not with him at the bridge or had been taken to a different location.

The state of Jake's foot brought into question the practicality of him climbing over the bridge's railings. Doing so, particularly at night and while in pain, would have been a substantial and slow effort, making it more probable for him to be noticed by passing drivers. Moreover, Jake's broken thumb further complicated the potential of such an action.

Given that Jake had firearms at home, it was perplexing as to why he would choose a method of suicide that was not only challenging but also painful, if indeed suicide was his intention. It is understood that individuals contemplating suicide might not think logically, yet the availability of more straightforward methods at his home made this scenario questionable.

Five years after Jake's disappearance, his aunt informed Tina that Jake's crutches had been in her shed the entire time. She claimed that Jake had told her he no longer needed them based on his doctor's advice. This revelation was strange for several reasons. The aunt had waited five years to disclose this information, despite the crutches being a focal point in the investigation from the beginning. Additionally, it contradicted the fact that Jake was awaiting foot surgery, suggesting he still needed the crutches.

In Jake's case, a pivotal detail emerged: he had a broken right foot and thumb at the time of his disappearance, rendering him reliant on crutches and an orthopedic boot, which he only removed for showering and dressing. Tina, Jake's mother, discovered his boot but not the crutches. If Jake had indeed jumped from the bridge, his body might have sunk, but the buoyant crutches would likely have floated, been spotted, or washed ashore. Their absence suggested they were not at the bridge or had been taken elsewhere.

Jake's broken foot raised doubts about his ability to climb over the bridge railings, especially at night and in pain. The effort required would have been significant, potentially attracting the attention of passing drivers. Adding to the complexity was Jake's broken thumb, making the feat even more challenging.

Given Jake's access to firearms at home, the choice of a challenging and painful method for a supposed suicide was perplexing. It seemed like an unnecessarily difficult option when more straightforward methods were available.

Five years later, a startling revelation came from Jake's aunt. She informed Tina that Jake's crutches had been in her shed all along, claiming he told her he no longer needed them following his doctor's advice. This was dubious, as Jake was awaiting foot surgery, indicating he still required the crutches. This delayed disclosure and contradiction added a new layer of complexity to the already mysterious case.

Throughout the investigation, Tina felt the authorities were disinterested, compelling her to take on the role of the primary investigator. She even went back to school for private investigation to seek justice for her son. People in the area knew to direct any new information about Jake's case to Tina, as law enforcement seemed uninvolved.

Tina collaborated with Ocean Open Source Intelligence, a company specializing in such cases, operating solely on facts. They expressed astonishment at the law enforcement's reluctance to act on the substantial intelligence gathered over five years, calling it a disservice to Jake's case and potential justice.

Focusing on the anonymous phone calls reported on the night of Jake's disappearance, Tina encountered inconsistencies. Initially, investigators claimed the calls were from a payphone, but no payphone was near the bridge. They then suggested a truck driver witnessed the fall and informed another driver who called it in, a claim that also seemed dubious.

Tina obtained 9-1-1 call recordings and easily identified the same number for both calls, indicating a single caller. She tried contacting the number herself, but the respondent denied any knowledge of the matter.

Examining Jake's phone records from the day before his disappearance raised further questions. The last text he received was around 11 pm, and his last call was to an unfamiliar number not saved in his contacts. This raised the possibility of Jake being in a distressed state, yet the nature of the call remained unclear.

Tina noted a change in the tone of Jake's text messages, leading her to believe someone else might have been sending them. Additionally, Jake's ex-girlfriend, with whom he had a child and was in a custody dispute, was not thoroughly investigated by the authorities, despite potentially being one of the last people to see him.

The case grew even more convoluted when Tina discovered stimulus checks in Jake's name being sent to an address in Mississippi linked to his ex-girlfriend's grandparents. This raised questions about the use of Jake's social security number and potential identity theft.

Many who knew Jake personally doubted he would have jumped off the bridge, and the lack of a found body only deepened the mystery. The authorities' unwillingness to thoroughly investigate, including not visiting his home or interviewing key individuals, left many unanswered questions.

Tina's mission to reopen Jake's case and conduct a proper investigation continues, as she spreads the word in hopes of uncovering more information. The circumstances surrounding Jake's disappearance remain a complex puzzle, with many pieces still missing.

Maureen Fields

estled 60 miles west of the dazzling lights and bustling streets of Las Vegas lies Pahrump, Nevada – a tranquil, unincorporated town that seems a world away from the neon glow of Sin City. Pahrump, cradled in the vast expanses of the Mojave Desert and not far from the California border, is a place where the pace of life slows, and the quiet of the desert holds sway. For many, Pahrump is the ideal location to retreat from the hustle and bustle of modern life, offering a serene backdrop for those seeking a peaceful retirement.

Among those drawn to this desert haven were Maureen and Paul Field, who in 2005 chose Pahrump as their sanctuary, a place to relish the quietude of their golden years. With the vibrant energy of Las Vegas just an hour's drive away, they found the perfect balance between tranquility and the occasional thrill.

But this serene existence was shattered in 2006, less than a year after their move. The aftermath of Valentine's Day, a time usually filled with the warmth of romantic memories, took a grim turn. In the desolate stretches near Death Valley, just across the California border, a green car was discovered abandoned. The scene, set against the barren landscape, was like a still from a mystery film.

The car, mired in the desert sands off a remote highway, was an eerie tableau. Inside, an array of items: an empty prescription bottle, religious pamphlets, a purse with cash still inside. The keys were in the ignition, a rifle in the back seat, and a pair of nylon pantyhose, ominously knotted, lay within. Outside, a blood-stained blanket lay sprawled on the sand.

Back in Pahrump, a mere 30 miles away, a separate but connected drama was unfolding. Maureen Fields, known for her punctuality and dedication, had not shown up for work. Concern rippled through her community – Maureen was not one to disappear without notice.

As the sheriff's deputies began their investigation, they unearthed a chilling premonition. Maureen, a woman of routine and reliability, had expressed a haunting fear to her friends and family: if she ever vanished, her husband was to be suspected.

To understand Maureen, one must look back to her beginnings. Born on November 16, 1964, to Jim and Barbara Fitzgerald, Maureen was the middle child, sandwiched between her older sister Kathleen and younger brother James. From a young age, she exhibited a nurturing spirit, always finding small ways to care for those around her.

Her early life was marked by the close bonds within her family. Her father, Jim, was a respected officer with the Newark Police Department, and her mother, a dedicated homemaker. However, when Maureen was 12, the family faced a seismic shift as her parents divorced. Despite this, both parents strove to maintain a strong connection with their children.

Jim eventually left the police force, remarried, and relocated to Randolph, a town 30 miles away. Maureen, meanwhile, attended North Arlington High School. There, she immersed herself in various clubs, notably the Club Panamericano, and her academic prowess earned her a spot in the National Honor Society. Despite this achievement, higher education was not in her plans; she was more practical, focusing on skills that would serve her immediately.

Mathematics was Maureen's forte. Her sister Kathleen recalled her exceptional talent in this area, evidenced by her active participation in the school's Math League. After graduating in 1983, Maureen parlayed her numerical aptitude into a career, securing positions at local banks, where her skills shone brightly.

In the pivotal year of 1983, transitioning into 1984, Maureen, at the tender age of 19, was about to embark on a significant chapter in her life. It was during this time that she would cross paths with Paul Fields, a man who would play a crucial role in her future. Paul, standing tall at six feet three inches and recognizable by his distinctive red hair, was affectionately known as "Big Red" among his acquaintances. His life journey diverged sharply from the conventional path; Paul left Bloomfield High School during his tenth-grade year and immediately ventured into the world of work, where he carved out a niche for himself.

Paul's entrepreneurial spirit led him to operate a small limousine service, a gas station, and even a rooming house. But his true passion lay in the realm of automobiles. He eventually found his calling in running his own shop, where he specialized in repairing and selling used cars. It was in this automotive world that Maureen and Paul's paths intertwined. According to Paul, their connection was instant and undeniable. Despite the significant age gap – Maureen was 19 and Paul was 34 – their relationship blossomed.

Maureen's family, however, harbored reservations about this relationship, primarily due to the substantial age difference between the two. Paul, having already experienced marriage, divorce, and fatherhood to two daughters, stood in stark contrast to Maureen's nascent journey into adulthood. Maureen, according to her sister, always had an affinity for older men, seeing in them a figure of stability and guidance.

In the early stages of their relationship, Paul's generosity towards Maureen was evident. He lavished her with gifts, including vehicles and jewelry, and indulged in vacations and cruises. This phase of largesse would culminate in their marriage in April 1991. At the time of their union, Maureen was 27, and Paul was 42. They exchanged vows in Northern New Jersey, where both had spent most of their lives.

Following their marriage, the couple decided to embark on a new adventure, relocating to Fort Myers, Florida. There, they spent 14 years building their life together. Paul continued his work in the automobile industry, while Maureen remained steadfast in her banking career. During these years, Paul managed to make astute real estate investments, which would later prove to be highly profitable.

The couple's fondness for Las Vegas was evident in their annual vacations to the city. On one such trip in the mid-90s, they contemplated relocating there. However, a conversation with a waitress introduced them to Pahrump, a small, serene town located 60 miles west of Las Vegas. Captivated by its blend of tranquility and proximity to the lively city, they decided to purchase land there.

As the 90s drew to a close, cracks began to appear in Maureen and Paul's marriage. Financial control became a contentious issue, with Paul allegedly taking a dominant role in their monetary affairs. Maureen's family claimed that he exerted such control over their finances that Maureen was compelled to surrender her paycheck to him. Paul, however, refuted these claims, insisting that Maureen had her own bank account and highlighting an instance where Maureen had to declare bankruptcy due to credit card debts.

Their troubles weren't confined to financial matters. Paul's jealousy over Maureen's interactions with others became increasingly apparent. Paula Camurata, a close friend of Maureen's, recounted how Paul's suspicion would flare whenever Maureen spent time outside their home. This jealousy was not just a private matter; it manifested publicly, such as during a cruise where Paul accused Maureen of flirting with a chef.

The situation escalated to the point where Maureen expressed genuine fear for her safety, worried that Paul's jealousy could lead to something more sinister.

Paula Camurata's concern for Maureen's well-being intensified as the couple planned their move to Pahrump, Nevada. Camurata vividly recalls trying to dissuade Maureen from relocating, fearing the consequences of living isolated in the desert with a husband she described as jealous and tyrannical. Initially, Maureen seemed enthusiastic about the new chapter in their lives, but as she mulled over the decision, doubt crept in, influenced by Camurata's warnings. Despite these reservations, Paul's determination prevailed, and the move was set in motion. Camurata still remembers the unsettling phone call from Paul, his voice ringing with triumph as he declared their impending move to Pahrump.

In April 2005, Maureen, then 40, and Paul, aged 55, embarked on their 2,500-mile journey from Florida to their new home in Pahrump. This move came at a time when both were grappling with health issues; Maureen was dealing with foot problems, necessitating surgery, and Paul had undergone a serious operation to remove his left lung due to lung cancer. They hoped this relocation would mark the beginning of a peaceful retirement.

Settling into a double-wide mobile home on the property Paul had purchased on North Leslie Street, they had plans to build a comfortable home for their retirement. However, county records revealed Paul's intentions to rezone the land for his used car business, hinting at divergent priorities within their marriage.

Months after their move, Maureen's sister Kathleen visited, hoping the change of scenery might have positively impacted their marital struggles. However, it became evident during her visit that the move had not eased their tensions. Kathleen recalls a poignant moment in the garage, away from Paul's earshot, where Maureen broke down, confessing that Paul had changed and she was struggling to cope with their marriage.

Adding to their marital strife was a new issue: gambling. Maureen had developed a penchant for video poker, which was quickly spiraling into an addiction. Their frequent dinners at low-cost buffets in local casinos provided Maureen ample opportunity to indulge in this new habit.

Amidst these challenges, Maureen took up a job as a bank teller at a local Wells Fargo. It was around this time she began voicing a haunting premonition to friends and family: if she ever disappeared, Paul was to be blamed.

In September 2005, Maureen surprised her family by announcing a solo visit to the East Coast, leaving Paul behind in Nevada. During her stay, she reconnected with old friends and confided in Kathleen her plans to divorce Paul. She expressed fear for her life, telling Kathleen of Paul's threats. Despite Kathleen's pleas to stay, Maureen was resolute about returning to Nevada, citing her new job, her beloved dog Wolfy, and her attachment to Pahrump.

Maureen believed that Nevada's community property divorce laws would entitle her to a significant portion of their assets, which had appreciated in value to nearly half a million dollars. She shared these plans with Paula Camurata, who, like Kathleen, advised against returning to Nevada.

During her visit, Maureen sought out Paul's daughter and brother, hoping to meet them. At a dinner gathering, she reiterated her ominous warning about Paul. Her brother James inquired about physical abuse, but Maureen assured him she had never been physically harmed by Paul. The evening, despite the heavy conversation, ended on a pleasant note.

On the morning of February 14, 2006, Maureen Fields arrived at her job at Wells Fargo on Highway 160, driving a green 2004 Hyundai – a recent Valentine's Day gift from her husband, Paul. This gesture might have hinted at a day of romance and celebration, yet Maureen's demeanor suggested otherwise. Known for her cheerful disposition and small acts of kindness like bringing donuts and bagels for her colleagues, Maureen was visibly distressed that day. Her colleagues couldn't help but notice her unusual mood; she was not just upset, but they sensed a deeper fear in her, an apprehension that seemed to go beyond everyday concerns.

During her shift, several bank employees noted Maureen's repeated expressions of anxiety, particularly about her husband, Paul. Her behavior was far from her typical, upbeat self, and she seemed preoccupied with the thought that something terrible might happen, implicating Paul in her fears.

An incident that afternoon further highlighted Maureen's distressed state. A woman from her church visited the bank, and during their interaction, Maureen's concern escalated. She reached out across the counter, gripping the woman's arm, conveying a sense of urgency and fear about Paul.

The last confirmed sighting of Maureen was around 5:30 PM that day, as she clocked out and drove away in her Hyundai. Scheduled to work the following morning, her absence raised immediate concerns among her colleagues, especially in light of her behavior the previous day.

By 8:30 AM on February 15th, when Maureen did not show up for work, her colleagues grew increasingly worried. After waiting for about 20 minutes, the bank management attempted to contact her at home but received no response. Eventually, they reached out to Paul. He informed them that Maureen had left for work at 8 AM, as usual, and he had not seen her since.

It's believed that later that day, Maureen's coworkers contacted the Nye County Sheriff's Office to report her missing. Initially, the investigators had little to go on, so they turned to Paul for information, as he was the last person to have seen Maureen that morning.

Paul recounted to the investigators that Maureen had been in considerable pain that morning, mentioning issues with her foot, which had undergone surgery, and back pain. He also shared concerns about her health, noting that she was worried about breast cancer, as her doctor had found lumps during an exam. However, according to Paul, Maureen was hesitant to get further tests. He added that she had been losing weight and had ignored a letter from her doctor urging her to get the lumps checked.

When asked about the likelihood of Maureen leaving voluntarily, Paul expressed doubts, mainly because she had left behind her beloved dog, Wolfy. Maureen's family echoed this sentiment, explaining to the police how much Wolfy meant to her. Unable to have children, Maureen had adopted Wolfy, an abandoned dog, and nurtured him back to health. She treated Wolfy like her child, often sending photos of him to her family and organizing playdates and birthday celebrations for him. Everyone who knew Maureen was certain she would never leave without Wolfy.

The investigators found Paul's behavior and responses during their inquiries to be unusual, raising suspicions. However, they lacked concrete evidence to prove any involvement or knowledge he might have had in Maureen's disappearance.

Authorities had only a description of the vehicle Maureen was last seen driving. Paul, her husband, and others were clueless about her whereabouts. Paul later claimed that he visited the sheriff's office to report Maureen missing after learning from the bank that she hadn't shown up for work. However, the sheriff's office stated that while Paul did visit, he didn't file a missing person report but merely inquired about a green Hyundai, leaving without mentioning his missing wife.

The case took a significant turn on the morning of February 16th when authorities in Inyo County, California, were alerted to an abandoned vehicle off Highway 178, between the Mojave Desert and Death Valley. The green Hyundai, found 150 feet off the main road and stuck in a wash, was approximately 10 miles west of the Nevada state line. This discovery suggested that the car had been deliberately driven off the road into the desert.

Upon examination, investigators found several peculiar items in and around the vehicle. The car keys were in the ignition, the driver's seat reclined back, and Maureen's purse, along with cash, credit cards, and religious pamphlets, was on the passenger seat. On the driver's side floorboard, neatly placed under the gas pedal, were a pair of slippers and glasses. An empty bottle of Xanax, which had contained 30 pills, was also found in the car. Additionally, a knotted pair of women's pantyhose raised further questions.

Outside the car, a blanket with apparent blood and vomit stains lay on the desert sand. A .22 caliber rifle was found in the back seat, a detail initially withheld from the public. The circumstances led to an early hypothesis that Maureen might have driven to the desert with self-harm intentions. This theory was bolstered by her alleged statements about not wanting to be in pain and the situation in which her car was found.

Search efforts were extensive, involving horseback patrols, ATVs, foot searches, helicopters, and tracking dogs. Despite the exhaustive search, no evidence of Maureen's presence in the desert was found – no footprints, clothing, or other indicators.

The initial theory of suicide began to unravel as the scene appeared increasingly staged. The religious pamphlets and the Xanax bottle, conspicuously wiped clean of fingerprints, suggested a deliberate attempt to mislead investigators.

The forensic analysis of the blanket confirmed that the blood and vomit were Maureen's, but the wiped-clean Xanax bottle raised suspicions of foul play. With these developments, the focus of the investigation turned towards Paul Fields. When police re-interviewed Paul, his account of the morning Maureen disappeared changed slightly. He mentioned an argument between them, but the details of this dispute remained unclear.

Paul's explanations, including his reference to Maureen's unlikely return to

New Jersey due to her affinity for her hair, struck investigators as odd. He reiterated his belief that Maureen wouldn't leave Wolfie, her cherished dog, further complicating the narrative.

During the second interview with investigators, Paul Fields faced questions about his firearms. He confirmed owning several guns, and when asked to check if any were missing, he found that his .22 caliber rifle was not in its usual place in the gun cabinet. He expressed doubt that Maureen would have taken the rifle, given its age and questionable functionality, and his belief that she was not familiar with its use. Detectives then revealed that the rifle had been found in the backseat of the Hyundai, but Paul couldn't explain how it got there or why Maureen would have taken it. This development intensified the focus on Paul, with investigators suspecting he knew more than he was letting on. They purposely gave him minimal details about the findings in and around the car.

Paul later expressed to the Pahrump Valley Times his frustration with being considered a suspect and the lack of information from the police. He lamented over Maureen's absence, noting her back problems and how they impacted her mobility.

Weeks after Maureen's disappearance, Paul contacted the Nye County Sheriff's Office with new information. He had received credit card bills in Maureen's name showing cash advances totaling nearly $8,000. Paul claimed he was unaware of these new credit cards, suggesting Maureen might have obtained them through her bank job. The sheriff's office confirmed receiving these bills from Paul but noted the amount was significantly less than $8,000.

In early March, Paul spoke with reporters, sharing his daily experience of returning home to an excited Wolfy, Maureen's dog, who was seemingly awaiting her return. He also mentioned not having any recent photos of Maureen, claiming she must have taken them when she disappeared. He had taken down the photos he did have, finding it too painful to look at them.

Paul maintained his lack of knowledge about Maureen's fate, portraying their relationship as harmonious. However, the investigation led to the questioning of 45-year-old Kenneth Robichaud, who was subsequently arrested for drug possession. The connection between Robichaud's arrest and Maureen's case remains unclear, with some speculating it might relate to the Xanax bottle found in her car.

Maureen's father, Jim, a former Newark police officer, and her sister Kathleen flew to Nevada to assist in the search. Jim met with Nye County Sheriff Tony DeMeo, and a bond was formed due to their shared New Jersey police background. DeMeo promised to do everything possible to find Maureen.

Lieutenant Ed Howard, leading the investigation, noted Paul's controlling nature. He found it peculiar that the Valentine's Day card Paul gave Maureen was addressed to "wife" rather than using her name. Jim's visit to Paul's home did not yield new information. The sheriff's office considered Paul the only suspect and noted contradictions in his statements. Paul refused a polygraph test, hired a lawyer, and ceased cooperating with the investigation.

Co-workers of Maureen offered to help Paul in the search, but he declined their assistance. The police confirmed that Paul did put up some missing person flyers, but his overall lack of cooperation raised suspicions. However, Paul did allow the police to search his property twice, though no evidence related to Maureen was found.

Jim confronted Paul about refusing the polygraph test, which Paul dismissed, citing mistrust of the police. Jim offered to pay for a private polygraph test, but Paul still refused. Jim's visit to the desert site where Maureen's car was found highlighted the challenges of searching in such terrain. The family even consulted a psychic but found no leads.

Kathleen speculated about Paul's motive, citing greed and their frugal lifestyle despite owning valuable land. Paul's actions only fueled the family's suspicions and law enforcement's interest. In May 2006, Paul filed to have Maureen's name removed from the deed to their land, claiming she had abandoned him. In response, Jim filed to become Maureen's legal guardian, countering Paul's attempt to claim sole ownership of their property.

As the legal battle over Maureen's guardianship continued, the investigation into her disappearance entered a quieter phase for almost two years. In February 2008, Nye County investigators reinvigorated public interest in the case by announcing new evidence, while expressing frustration at Paul Fields' lack of cooperation since he had retained an attorney.

Investigators delved into Paul's past, interviewing his first wife, Linda, in New Jersey. Linda described their five-year marriage as volatile, marked by child support disputes and mysterious incidents of vandalism she suspected were Paul's doing, although she couldn't prove it. Paul admitted to retaliating against Linda's new partner but denied vandalizing her car. Linda clarified that while Paul was troublesome, he was not physically abusive, except for one instance where a confrontation led to her receiving a black eye.

Paul's daughters from his first marriage expressed estrangement and fear of their father, with one stating she would call the police if he appeared at her doorstep. Linda, concerned for her safety, requested her new married name be withheld from the press.

Paul, when questioned about Maureen's disappearance, speculated she might have run off with a lover, staging the desert scene to appear as a suicide. He defended his actions towards Maureen, questioning why he would harm her after all he had done for her.

In a strategic legal move, Paul filed to have Maureen declared legally dead less than three years after her disappearance, citing Nevada law that allows for such a declaration based on testimony from those most likely to hear from the missing person. On July 6, 2009, Maureen was officially declared dead, and Paul was named the administrator of her estate, gaining complete legal ownership of all properties and assets. However, the judge ordered the couple's assets frozen for an additional year due to the suspicious circumstances of her disappearance.

Maureen's father, Jim, attempted to file a wrongful death lawsuit against Paul, but the statute of limitations had expired. Frustrated, Jim criticized Nye County prosecutor Robert Beckett for not moving forward with charges despite circumstantial evidence linking Paul to Maureen's disappearance. Beckett's reluctance was attributed to the high stakes of election-based prosecution rates, leading to a preference for 'slam dunk' cases.

Jim's efforts to meet with D.A. Beckett were unsuccessful, as Beckett cited a lack of appointment scheduling. Beckett maintained that without substantial evidence, charges could not be filed, citing the finality of a not guilty verdict due to double jeopardy laws.

Sheriff DeMeo reaffirmed their belief in Paul Fields as the prime suspect, despite the lack of DNA or fingerprints directly linking him to the crime. Meanwhile, D.A. Beckett revealed during a CNN interview that DNA had been recovered from key items in Maureen's car, although details about the DNA tests or potential matches were not disclosed, much to the frustration of the sheriff's office.

In October 2009, Texas-based search organization EquuSearch conducted a search of the desert area near where Maureen's car was found. Assisted by the sheriff's office, this renewed search effort aimed to uncover new evidence or leads that could bring closure to Maureen's case.

EquuSearch, an experienced search and rescue organization, employed sophisticated drones to scan the rugged desert terrain, while the Sheriff's Office complemented these efforts with ground searches using canines, horseback units, and four-wheel ATVs. Part of the search encompassed a section of land in the Pahrump Valley, including property owned by Paul Fields. Paul had consented to the search of his land, though he restricted access to inside his home.

Tim Miller from EquuSearch explained the effectiveness of drones in previous searches. These drones could fly at significant altitudes, scanning the landscape and relaying information back to a computer system. This technology helped detect disturbances in the earth's surface, such as sunken or swollen areas, potentially indicating a grave or other significant findings. Despite their advanced methods and a $10,000 reward for information about Maureen's whereabouts, these extensive searches yielded no new evidence or leads.

Meanwhile, the investigation into Maureen's disappearance had hit a standstill. With only circumstantial evidence pointing to Paul Fields and no solid evidence for prosecution, the case remained unsolved. However, public attention in Pahrump shifted to a different matter involving District Attorney Robert Beckett and the Sheriff's Office.

In April 2010, the Sheriff's Office executed a search warrant at Beckett's office, seizing accounting records related to a fund for prosecuting bad check cases. This action stemmed from concerns raised by the County Treasurer and Auditor about unaccounted funds. Their findings suggested financial irregularities, including several thousand dollars worth of cashed checks with no clear record of their expenditure. One of the checks was noted to have been donated to the Pahrump Valley High School cheer squad, where Beckett's daughters were members and his wife the coach.

Beckett was arrested on charges of embezzlement, fraud, and public misconduct. He denied any wrongdoing, alleging political motivations behind his arrest. The case presented legal complexities, as Beckett couldn't oversee his own case and both judges in Nevada's Fifth Judicial District had conflicts of interest.

In response to his arrest, Beckett appointed a special prosecutor to investigate Detective David Berokowicz, who had arrested him. Berokowicz was later cleared of all charges due to a lack of evidence. Beckett's legal battles continued, including a DUI arrest and an eventual plea agreement that led to his resignation and the dismissal of his charges.

By February 2012, six years after Maureen's disappearance, the case had seen no significant developments. The Nye County Sheriff's Office still viewed Paul Fields as a person of interest, but no charges had been filed. Maureen's father, Jim, remained convinced of Paul's involvement, citing circumstantial evidence. New District Attorney Brian Kunzie had not been provided with evidence warranting prosecution and had not yet communicated with Maureen's family.

In October 2012, the case took a dramatic turn when Detective Berokowicz, now leading the investigation, confirmed that DNA had been found on the knotted pantyhose in Maureen's car. The discovery of skin cells on the pantyhose led to questions about whether the DNA belonged to a suspect or to rescue workers who had accessed the car. The Sheriff's Office was seeking warrants to obtain DNA from these workers, as the sample had not been initially run through the FBI's Combined DNA Index System (CODIS).

Two months earlier, Berokowicz had submitted the DNA sample to CODIS, and it resulted in an immediate hit.

The revelation that the DNA found in Maureen Field's car belonged to Keith Wayne Holmes, an 81-year-old convicted sex offender from Southern California, significantly complicated the investigation. Holmes had a criminal history, including attempts to lure a child into his car and convictions for child molestation. Despite his denial of any knowledge of Maureen, Paul Fields, or the circumstances surrounding her disappearance, his presence in Pahrump around the time of her vanishing added a new layer of mystery to the case.

Investigators had met with Paul Fields to discuss the DNA match in an attempt to unearth any possible connection between him and Holmes. However, Paul preemptively disclosed this information to the media, emphasizing that the DNA found did not match his own. This move by Paul was driven by his frustration at being the sole suspect for years and his desire to highlight that there were other potential leads in the case.

Sheriff DeMayo, acknowledging the release of this information, explained the decision to keep the DNA match confidential initially was to follow up on leads related to Holmes and trace his activities in the Pahrump Valley. The Sheriff's Office aimed to provide accurate information based on evidence rather than speculation.

Former District Attorney Beckett acknowledged the existence of the unknown DNA in the car, including on the stocking, and stated that this was a major reason for not filing charges against Paul. However, Beckett emphasized that while the DNA pointed towards Holmes, it did not entirely exonerate Paul. Contradictory statements made by Paul and questionable phone records from the night of Maureen's disappearance continued to cast doubt on his innocence.

Detective Berokowicz's investigation into Keith Holmes revealed a disturbing pattern of behavior. Holmes had been arrested for trying to lure a 12-year-old child into his car, and a search of his vehicle had uncovered rope and duct tape, which he claimed were for boat repairs. Holmes, who admitted to visiting Pahrump for vacations, had no clear reason for his trips, and his statements were deemed theatrical and not very informative.

Investigators were intrigued by the similarity between Paul's 1964 Ford camper and Holmes' 1965 model, speculating a potential connection through the sale or repair of used cars. However, Paul denied selling used cars since moving to Pahrump, despite rezoning his land for that purpose.

Holmes' trips to Pahrump began in 2006, and locals who had encountered him described him as a polite man who often sang church songs. Initially accompanied by his wife, Holmes later visited alone for reasons unknown. Attempts to establish a motive for Holmes' visits were inconclusive, as he had no connections to local brothels or casinos.

Investigators couldn't establish a definitive link between Holmes and Paul Fields, Maureen's husband, who remained a key figure in the investigation. Detective Berokowicz emphasized that the investigation was still open, and no one, including Paul, had been cleared.

Paul Fields expressed his frustration at being the primary focus of the investigation for years. He believed that if the police had diverted their attention from him earlier, they might have uncovered Holmes' potential involvement sooner. Despite questioning Paul multiple times, investigators maintained that his actions and statements gave them reason to suspect his involvement.

Maureen's father, Jim, was hopeful that the new lead would bring some resolution to the case. He speculated that if Paul had been more cooperative from the beginning, perhaps the link to Holmes would have been established earlier.

The case hit a standstill with the new DNA evidence. Investigators couldn't charge Holmes with a crime, nor could they take any action against Paul. They continued to explore possible connections between Holmes and Maureen or Holmes and Paul, but the leads were elusive.

Holmes, who admitted crossing paths with Maureen on the day she disappeared, claimed they had consensual sex, but his declining mental state made his statements unreliable. His worsening condition and eventual death left many questions unanswered. Intriguingly, a cut-out news article about Maureen's disappearance was found in Holmes' truck, suggesting he knew more than he had revealed.

Paul Fields criticized the investigation, claiming that the failure to submit the DNA to the FBI originally was not an oversight but a deliberate attempt to frame him. He speculated about Holmes' potential role in Maureen's disappearance, including the possibility of sexual assault or human trafficking.

Investigators continued to scrutinize Paul, highlighting discrepancies in his statements and actions. For instance, the .22 caliber rifle found in Maureen's car was a point of contention. Paul's explanation that he had given the rifle to Maureen to have it repaired was new information to the investigators.

Cell phone records contradicted Paul's claim of being home on the night Maureen disappeared. The records indicated that his phone was active in an area far from their house, raising further suspicions about his whereabouts that night.

Investigators theorized a possible connection between Paul and Holmes, perhaps through the sale of a used vehicle or another unknown link. They speculated that Paul might have enlisted Holmes' help in disposing of Maureen's body, considering Paul's physical limitations.

Paul Fields has consistently denied any involvement in his wife's disappearance. He argued that the focus on him hindered the investigation, leading to missed opportunities in pursuing other suspects.

The case remains unsolved. Detective Berokowicz has to annually re-add Maureen's name to the national missing person's database, reflecting the unique status of her case as alive, missing, and officially declared dead. Maureen, last seen alive on February 14, 2006, at Wells Fargo Bank in Nevada, was 41 years old at the time of her disappearance. She had a titanium surgical implant in her jaw, a distinctive identifier in the ongoing search for answers in her mysterious disappearance.

Daniel Robinson

Daniel Robinson's disappearance on June 23, 2021, at the age of 24, is a story that is as tragic as it is mystifying. Born in Columbia, South Carolina, Daniel was a young man of exceptional character and resilience. Despite being born with only one hand, with his other arm not developing beyond the forearm, Daniel never saw himself as limited or handicapped. His parents, especially his father David Robinson, recall how Daniel was a force of nature from a young age, always eager to take on new challenges and fiercely independent.

Rejecting the idea of using prosthetics, Daniel wanted to prove to the world and to himself that he could thrive just as he was. He dove into various activities with gusto, playing instruments like the trumpet and French horn, experimenting with sports like football and weightlifting, though his true passion lay in his academic pursuits. His intellect and curiosity led him to the College of Charleston, where he discovered a love for geology during his freshman year. This love wasn't a fleeting passion but a deep-seated interest that drove him to excel academically, culminating in his graduation with honors.

Daniel's journey as a geologist took him to Arizona, where he worked for Matrix New World Engineering. His role involved assessing the viability of water wells, a job that he not only excelled in but truly loved. Arizona's landscape was a geologist's dream, and Daniel eagerly awaited the opportunity to share its wonders with his family back in South Carolina. He had plans for his family's visit in July and a hiking trip with his sister the weekend following his mysterious disappearance.

However, beneath this façade of a well-adjusted and successful young professional lay unanswered questions. On the fateful day of his disappearance, Daniel's behavior was noted as peculiar by his coworker Ken. Ken observed Daniel acting out of character, talking nonsensically, and making unusual requests. This behavior was alarming enough for Ken to contact their supervisor, expressing his concern.

The subsequent events only deepen the mystery. According to Ken, only 15 minutes after arriving at the worksite in Buckeye, Arizona, Daniel abruptly left in his 2017 blue-gray Jeep Renegade. This sudden departure was the last confirmed sighting of Daniel. The efforts to find him intensified, with his father David piecing together Daniel's movements using cell phone and Google Maps data. It appeared Daniel had been working late the night before as an Instacart driver, suggesting he might have been extremely tired on the morning of his disappearance.

The investigation into Daniel's disappearance revealed inconsistencies and raised more questions than answers. Ken's changing account of the events and the lack of direct communication with Daniel after his departure only added to the confusion and concern. David's realization that no one, including Daniel's sister and mother, had heard from him all day was alarming, considering the close-knit nature of their family.

Daniel, known for his unwavering spirit and determination, was a figure whose sudden absence sent shockwaves through his close-knit circle. His father, David, stationed far away in South Carolina, was immediately alarmed by the uncharacteristic silence from his son. In a desperate bid to glean some insight into Daniel's whereabouts, David reached out to Daniel's sister, who lived in Arizona, the only immediate family member in the vicinity. She lived in stark contrast to another sister in California, with the rest of their family rooted back in South Carolina.

Upon David's urgent request, Daniel's sister rushed to his Tempe apartment, only to be met with the unsettling reality that Daniel was nowhere to be found. David's anxiety intensified, leading him to contact one of Daniel's friends, but to no avail; they too had not heard from Daniel. As the hours ominously ticked by, with over six hours passing since Daniel was last seen, David took the decisive step of reporting his son as missing to the Buckeye police. Without hesitation, David embarked on a grueling thirty-hour, two-thousand-mile drive from South Carolina to Buckeye, Arizona.

Initially, the police response seemed lackluster, their efforts not matching the gravity of the situation. It wasn't until the next day, June 24th, that the investigation seemed to gain some momentum. A Tempe police officer dispatched to Daniel's apartment left without entering when there was no answer, a move that further complicated the situation. On the same day, David's request for a helicopter search was initially dismissed, with the police suggesting that Daniel, as an adult, might have chosen to disappear. This standard response, often given in missing person cases, did little to assuage the family's fears.

Persistence from Daniel's family eventually led to the authorization of a helicopter search, but doubts lingered about its thoroughness. David's arrival in the search area marked a turning point, with over 20 volunteers joining the search, yet Daniel remained elusive. Efforts to locate him through cell phone pings were futile, and although some cell phone records were obtained, they revealed no communication from Daniel after he left the job site.

The breakthrough in the case came nearly a month later on July 19th, when a ranger, using a drone, discovered Daniel's jeep overturned in a ravine, badly damaged, and only three miles from his work site. This discovery raised critical questions about the effectiveness of the police search – if a ranger could locate the jeep with a drone, why couldn't the police find it during their helicopter search? The police attributed their oversight to the challenging terrain and the jeep's obscured location.

At the crash site, a peculiar scene unfolded: Daniel's jeans, work boots, an orange vest with his company logo, a t-shirt, and socks – all found outside the jeep and inside out. Inside the jeep were Daniel's wallet, cell phone, keys, and his backpack containing his work laptop. Strikingly, there was no blood or signs of a severe injury within the car. This discovery, while concerning, provided a new direction for the search.

Despite an extensive search involving officers and cadaver dogs for 18 hours, no trace of Daniel was found. Frustrated by the lack of progress, Daniel's family hired a private investigator to delve deeper into the case. Both the Buckeye police and the private investigator analyzed the car's black box data, yet they arrived at conflicting conclusions. While the original police report indicated that the collision's date and time were not recorded, the private investigator determined that the crash occurred around 1 PM on the day Daniel was last seen, approximately four hours after his last sighting.

The data suggested that the driver, who was wearing a seatbelt at the time of the crash, had accelerated before the collision, possibly attempting to drive up the other side of the ravine.

The vehicle's black box data revealed a harrowing tale: the jeep had rolled over multiple times and was immobilized, yet there were more than 40 ignition attempts post-crash, suggesting someone had tried to restart the vehicle at least 43 times after the airbags deployed. But the mystery deepened with an 11-mile discrepancy between the crash data and the jeep's odometer readings. While police brushed this off as a common issue reported at other Jeep dealerships, the family's private investigator (PI) was not convinced.

The PI's findings contradicted the official narrative. He argued that there was no evidence the car sped up before the crash, and even conducted his own experiment to challenge the police's theory. His results indicated it was impossible to reach 30 mph on that terrain. Moreover, the additional 11 miles logged after the airbag deployment hinted at a more sinister possibility: the jeep might have been driven to its final location after an initial crash elsewhere. This was supported by red paint transfer on the vehicle, suggesting a collision with an object not typically found in the desert, and by the type of damage which was more consistent with a head-on collision rather than a rollover.

These findings raised serious questions about the circumstances surrounding the crash. Why was there a four-hour gap between Daniel being last seen and the time of the crash, especially when his car was found just three miles from his worksite? The PI speculated that the scene could have been staged, a theory that gained traction due to the lack of a thorough forensic examination of the jeep by the police.

Amidst these developments, more information about Daniel's state of mind in the days leading up to his disappearance surfaced. Friends, co-workers, and family members recounted unusual behaviors, though the accuracy of these reports was questionable, with discrepancies between what was recorded in the police report and what David, Daniel's father, claimed. One such instance involved Daniel's social media activity, specifically the deletion of all posts from his Instagram account. The timing of this action remained unclear, with conflicting reports on whether it occurred before or after his disappearance.

Additionally, there were revelations about a woman named Caitlyn, whom Daniel had met while working for Instacart. His father described a connection between the two, but the nature of their relationship and its impact on Daniel's mental state was not fully understood. Furthermore, there were conflicting accounts of Daniel's behavior during a visit to his sister's apartment. While the police report suggested a prolonged, unresponsive state, David questioned the accuracy of this duration.

Daniel's sister also mentioned a Christian podcast recommended by Caitlyn that had profoundly influenced Daniel, changing his perspective on life. This new spiritual outlook, while seemingly positive, added another layer to the complex portrait of Daniel in the days leading up to his mysterious disappearance.

The police report introduced a compelling twist: it claimed that Daniel had confessed to his sister about being in love with a girl named Caitlyn. This assertion, however, was met with skepticism by David, Daniel's father, who doubted the veracity of this claim. The only tangible connection between Daniel and Caitlyn was a podcast he had mentioned, beyond which his sister did not recall any significant changes in his behavior or any indications of distress or desire to leave.

Adding layers to this narrative were the accounts of Daniel's friends. One friend recalled a conversation on June 16th where Daniel seemed unusually energetic and spoke about meeting two girls while delivering alcohol, allegedly becoming intimate with one. Yet, in a subsequent conversation on June 22nd, nothing seemed amiss; they simply discussed vacation spots in Arizona and California.

Another friend, considering relocating to Arizona and who had visited Daniel until June 20th, also reported nothing unusual about Daniel's demeanor. They shared a moment of camaraderie, captured in a photo with a caption celebrating the Suns in the playoffs, further dispelling any notions of Daniel being troubled.

David, too, had spoken with Daniel shortly before his disappearance. Their conversation revolved around everyday topics, including the podcast Daniel had discovered. Daniel had inquired about love, a seemingly innocent query from someone who had not ventured much into the realms of romance. David recalled Daniel mentioning a girl he met while working for Instacart but nothing to suggest a deep emotional involvement.

However, the police report painted a different picture, alleging that Daniel confessed to being in love with Caitlyn during this call – a claim David firmly denied. According to David, Daniel had merely sought fatherly advice about love, without delving deeply into his feelings for this girl.

The enigmatic figure of Caitlyn loomed large in this narrative. Daniel had indeed mentioned her to friends and family, but the extent of their relationship appeared exaggerated in the police report. Caitlyn herself, when interviewed by the police, clarified that their acquaintance was brief and not romantic. They had met on June 12th when she and a friend, both inebriated, invited Daniel inside after he delivered their Instacart order. Caitlyn admitted that inviting a stranger into their home might not have been prudent, but at the moment, Daniel seemed harmless and congenial.

Their interaction led to Daniel spending the night, during which Caitlyn shared the podcast link with him. Subsequent text exchanges between Daniel and Caitlyn were sporadic, with the police report only presenting a selective view of their communication, as Caitlyn was allowed to upload the messages she chose.

The canopy left at Caitlyn's house became a focal point of their texts. Daniel's attempts to retrieve it led to an unannounced visit to her house, observed via her security system, as she was out of town and did not respond to his request for directions.

Caitlyn's discomfort began to grow when Daniel unexpectedly visited her house without explicit permission. Although she had previously told him he could come and collect the canopy left at her place, she hadn't specified a particular day for his visit. Her surprise was heightened when Daniel found her house without directions from her, leading her to suspect he might have retraced his route through Instacart.

The situation escalated on June 16th when Caitlyn confronted Daniel about showing up uninvited, as seen on her security footage. Her message was clear: she would inform him when she was back in town to arrange a time for him to retrieve the canopy. Despite offering to leave it out for him, Daniel's subsequent messages veered into unsettling territory. He responded with a heart emoji, declaring his love for her, a sentiment Caitlyn did not reciprocate. Daniel's apology message later that evening further complicated the narrative.

Daniel's continued unannounced visits despite Caitlyn's requests not to do so only intensified her unease. The text messages, as per the police report, revealed a one-sided conversation with Daniel expressing affection and Caitlyn expressing discomfort. The exchanges lacked timestamps, creating gaps that made the context of messages like "I can't stop thinking about you" difficult to discern.

Caitlyn's unease turned into discomfort and then alarm as Daniel persisted in his unannounced visits and declarations of love, even after she explicitly told him she was uncomfortable. The conversation culminated in a series of texts where Caitlyn firmly stated her boundaries, leaving no ambiguity about her feelings. Daniel's texts in response, asking for reassurance and attempting to understand 'normal' social interactions, underscored the complexity of the situation.

As the days progressed, Daniel's messages continued, oscillating between seeking approval and acknowledging Caitlyn's discomfort. His last message to Caitlyn, sent the day before his disappearance, was cryptic and poignant, hinting at a troubled state of mind. The lack of a response from Caitlyn left these final words hanging in the air.

The narrative, as presented, suggests a one-sided emotional attachment from Daniel, marked by repeated uninvited visits to Caitlyn's home and declarations of affection. However, the authenticity and completeness of these messages are in question. Caitlyn had the autonomy to choose which texts to share with the police, potentially omitting crucial parts of their conversation. This selective reporting casts doubt on the full context of their interactions.

David, Daniel's father, acknowledges that his son, having never been in a serious relationship, might not have fully grasped the nuances of romantic boundaries. Daniel's repeated visits to Caitlyn's house, ostensibly to retrieve his canopy, could be seen as naivety rather than malice. However, his persistence, especially after being explicitly told his actions were making Caitlyn uncomfortable, complicates the picture. Was Daniel simply unaware of the impact of his actions, or was there something more troubling at play?

The police report's portrayal of Daniel as overly persistent might not capture the entire story. The need for his canopy, possibly for work purposes, suggests practical reasons for his visits, but the romantic overtones in his messages to Caitlyn paint a different picture. It's a nuanced situation, one where Daniel's intentions and Caitlyn's discomfort intersect in a way that is not entirely clear.

Amidst these personal complexities, the mystery of Daniel's disappearance deepens. A Tempe police officer's visit to Daniel's apartment on July 6th revealed no signs of foul play or intention to leave for an extended period. The only notable finding was the presence of legally owned marijuana, which offered no significant insight into his disappearance.

Further investigations led to a Waffle House Daniel visited on June 22nd, the day before he went missing. Surveillance footage showed him eating alone, and an employee noted that he seemed 'off' that day, although she couldn't pinpoint why. David, however, contested the employee's claim that Daniel was a regular customer, stating he had only been there a couple of times. This discrepancy adds another layer of uncertainty to Daniel's state of mind and actions leading up to his disappearance.

The last known communication from Daniel was a text to his sister on the night of June 22nd, simply stating 'emergency.' This text message that Daniel sent to his sister, which was a part of their sibling code for help, turned out to be a test of her response time, seemingly a light-hearted moment amidst the growing complexity of his life.

However, conversations with friends and co-workers revealed a different side of Daniel. Roger, a friend from college who had once invited Daniel to live with him in Arizona, noticed changes in Daniel's behavior upon his return from dealing with family issues. Daniel's unexpected presence in the office, a deviation from his usual fieldwork, and a surprising haircut marked a departure from his normal routine. Their breakfast together led to a conversation about belief in miracles and the power of faith, topics that Roger found unusual for Daniel to discuss, despite knowing his Christian upbringing.

Daniel's discussion with Roger about ego and personal narratives echoed themes from the podcast he was listening to, suggesting a deep impact on his mindset. Yet, these changes in behavior and conversation topics did not necessarily indicate anything ominous on their own. It seemed Daniel was exploring new perspectives, perhaps influenced by the podcast's themes on ego and personal transformation.

Meanwhile, David, Daniel's father, was growing increasingly frustrated with the police investigation. His military background and determination drove him to conduct his own investigation, staying in Arizona to be closer to the search efforts. David's conviction that the police had prematurely given up on his son fueled his relentless pursuit for answers, organizing regular search efforts with volunteers.

During these searches, led by David and their private investigator, they stumbled upon grim discoveries – human remains, including a skull and bones, scattered across the desert. These remains, however, were not connected to Daniel. One finding even led to a potential lead in another missing person's case, as a woman reached out to the PI suspecting the remains might belong to her missing husband.

The journey of searching for Daniel became a testament to a father's un-wavering hope and dedication. Despite the odds and the lack of substantial leads, David held onto the belief that he would one day reunite with his son. The discovery of the other human remains, while not providing closure for Daniel's case, underscored the harsh realities of the search and the possible outcomes.

David's frustration with the police findings, which differed significantly from his own, only intensified his resolve. He and his team continued their exhaustive searches, reaching out to the community for assistance, driven by the hope that Daniel's story would not end in the vast expanse of the Arizona desert, but with a father's embrace and the answers they so desperately sought.

Luke Joly-Durocher

In the scenic northeast region of Ontario, Canada, you'll find North Bay, a picturesque city situated on Lake Nipissing's northern shores. Since its foundation in 1891, North Bay has evolved into a vibrant center of commerce and history, gaining recognition for its vital railroad industry and as a key airbase during the Cold War.

Positioned about 300 kilometers from Ottawa and Toronto, North Bay offers a harmonious mix of city amenities and natural splendor.

Yet, behind its tranquil facade, North Bay has grappled with challenges. Recent years have seen a disturbing escalation in criminal activities, with a rise in overall crime, violent and property crimes, exceeding national averages. This trend encompasses concerning patterns in disappearances and drug-related offenses, yet the city remains known as the 'Gateway to the North,' highlighting its resilience and promise.

In this backdrop, Luke's story unfolds. Born on June 28, 1990, in Timiskaming, Quebec, a picturesque town at Lac Temiskaming's southern tip and the seat of the Algonquin Nation Wolf Lake First Nations band government, Luke's upbringing was warm and supportive. Raised by his parents, Rob and Monique, along with his sisters Priscilla and a younger sibling, Luke developed into a kind-hearted individual.

Those who knew Luke remember him as a beacon of kindness, always treating others with sincerity and compassion. Music was his passion, evident from the age of three when he first held a guitar. Dreaming of musical stardom, he was actively engaged in a band, dedicating himself wholeheartedly to his craft.

Luke, along with his friend Brett, ventured to North Bay to celebrate a friend's move to her own apartment. Despite Brett's reservations about the somewhat neglected neighborhood of the apartment at 683 Sherbrooke Street, they remained focused on the festivities.

The celebration moved to Cecil's Brewhouse and Kitchen, a well-known downtown bar, as the night advanced. Amidst the vibrant energy of Cecil's, they suddenly realized Luke was missing. This unexpected absence cast a perplexing shadow over the evening. Oddly, no one from the group went outside to search for Luke, a puzzling reaction considering his unfamiliarity with the city and the potential risks involved.

The subsequent events added layers of intrigue to the unfolding drama. Surveillance footage from that fateful night showed Luke being turned away from Cecil's, with suggestions of his inebriation often cited as the cause, yet no official explanation was ever confirmed. The CCTV captured him leaving at 11:54 PM, alone, a haunting final glimpse as he vanished into the night.

Earlier, at 8:51 PM, Luke's ordinary text to his father about a ride home from North Bay the next day stood in stark contrast to the ensuing mystery. His absence from the apartment post-celebration caused only minor confusion initially.

Concern escalated the following day when Luke missed his scheduled bus trip. Frantic communications between Brett and Luke's family ensued. Luke's mother, intuitively alarmed, considered contacting the police, but the family held back, clinging to hope.

Days passed with no word from Luke, his absence from his younger sister's birthday signaling a dire situation. Three days post-disappearance, his mother arrived in North Bay, confronting a heartrending scene at the friend's apartment: Luke's personal effects - phone, hoodie, jacket, keys, and glasses - lay abandoned, silent witnesses to his sudden absence. She collected these items and reported him missing to the police.

The family's distress was met with a perceived lack of urgency from the police. Authorities suggested Luke might have left voluntarily, a notion at odds with his character. A week later, a passerby found Luke's bank card in a snowbank, its last use a twenty-dollar withdrawal the day before he disappeared. This led to a police-conducted ground search, but it brought no closer to solving the mystery of Luke's disappearance.

The family's disillusionment grew as the police took an astonishing six weeks to search the apartment where Luke had stayed, a move that seemed both inexplicable and disheartening. When the search was finally conducted, the police were tight-lipped about any findings, leaving the family and public in the dark.

As the case progressed, communication from law enforcement waned, suggesting either a cooling trail or diminished investigative vigor. The situation remained stagnant until a pivotal moment months later: a 31-year-old woman came forward, claiming knowledge of Luke's murder, even pinpointing where his body could be found. Her detailed account led to extensive searches, but eventually, it was deemed a fabrication, resulting in her prosecution for obstruction and public mischief.

This misleading lead had significant consequences. It not only misdirected critical investigative efforts but also instilled fear and caution among potential informants, deterring them from sharing information for fear of legal consequences. Additionally, her concocted story muddled the investigation, influencing subsequent tips and complicating the process of distinguishing credible information.

Frustrated with the official investigation's lack of progress, independent efforts emerged. One such pursuit involved Luke's father, Rob, who tirelessly sought answers. He recently teamed up with Ellen White, a seasoned private investigator, offering a glimmer of hope in a case shrouded in uncertainty.

Simultaneously, 'Please Bring Me Home,' a group endorsed by Luke's mother, Monique, has been diligently working to solve the mystery. Their dedication underscores the community's impact from Luke's disappearance.

In North Bay, Luke's story is well-known, sparking widespread speculation. The prevailing belief is that Luke, who showed no signs of depression or suicidal intent, likely encountered foul play, casting doubt on his survival.

Years of evidence collection and analysis, including interviews and tips, have started to paint a consistent picture of Luke's last night. Approximately 90% of the received tips point to a similar chain of events. A notable tip suggests a tragic turn of events on Sherbrooke Street, where Luke, after leaving the bar, was allegedly involved in a street fight that led to his demise.

The investigation into Luke's disappearance took a haunting turn when a tipster suggested the fatal argument that led to his vanishing was over a mere twenty dollars – the same amount Luke had withdrawn before he went missing. This eerie coincidence lent an air of credibility to the account.

Recently, Rob and Ellen, following this lead, revisited the apartment to inspect a hidden crawl space. The property's owners cooperated, allowing them to search. Although initially unfruitful, another informant directed them to a concealed hatch in the crawl space, rumored to have been where Luke's body was temporarily hidden.

The discovery of the hatch, while not yielding direct evidence, supported the various narratives that have emerged over the years, suggesting a potential cover-up.

Many argue that the evidence gathered thus far should suffice for legal action, but, frustratingly, no charges have been made. There's speculation that initial investigative errors by the police may have hindered the case's progression.

The police, however, assert they have devoted considerable resources to the investigation. They note that in complex cases like Luke's, certain details must remain confidential.

On the fifth anniversary of Luke's disappearance, a $50,000 reward was announced for information leading to a resolution, yet it remains unclaimed, highlighting the elusive truth in this case.

In March 2023, Brett from the "Please Bring Me Home" group revealed they had gathered significant new evidence, including eyewitness accounts, details about the disposal of Luke's belongings, and even a purported confession. Reports also emerged of a mental health professional possessing a complete account of the incident.

Despite these revelations, the case remains stagnant, leaving those involved in a limbo of expectation and unresolved grief.

The consensus among investigators and informants is strong regarding the circumstances and perpetrators of Luke's disappearance. Yet, converting this consensus into legally admissible evidence remains a challenge.

At the time of his disappearance, Luke was 20, about 5 feet 8 inches tall, weighing around 150 pounds, with dark hair and brown eyes. He was last seen wearing jeans, black sneakers, an American Eagle pea coat, and a distinctive purple belt. Any information that could clarify Luke Joly-Durocher's fate would be invaluable, offering his family and community the closure and justice they have long sought.

Gwendolyn Brunelle

Gwendolyn Margaret "Gwen" Brunelle, a vivacious and talented young woman, was born on a chilly winter day, December 9, 1995, to the loving and proud parents Betsy and Andy Brunelle. From a very young age, Gwen displayed a unique and consuming passion for the animal kingdom, specifically focusing her energies on raising and showing purebred rabbits. This wasn't just a hobby for Gwen; it became a significant part of her identity and a source of great pride for her family.

Gwen's journey with rabbits began in the warm, community-focused environment of 4H, where she quickly distinguished herself as a prodigious talent. Her dedication and skill culminated in a remarkable achievement in 2007 when, at the tender age of 12, she was crowned Showmanship Champion at the prestigious Western Idaho Fair. This victory was not just a testament to her commitment but also a launching pad for her soaring ambitions.

Driven by her early success, Gwen set her sights on the national stage. She entered the highly competitive arena of the American Rabbit Breeders Association, where her talents continued to shine. In 2011, at the age of 16, she reached the pinnacle of her young career when she was honored with the title of Queen at the national competition – a recognition that placed her among the elite in the rabbit breeding community.

Amidst her rising acclaim in the rabbit show world, Gwen harbored a dream of becoming a certified rabbit judge, an aspiration that showcased her deepening commitment to her passion. She was tirelessly working towards this goal, balancing her personal ambitions with the demands of her everyday life.

However, Gwen's journey was not without its challenges. Behind her achievements and her bright, engaging personality, she struggled with a personal condition that often left her moody and inattentive. She faced this challenge with the same determination that she applied to her rabbit breeding, taking medication and striving to manage its impact on her life.

The days leading up to Gwen's mysterious disappearance were seemingly ordinary. On June 26, 2023, she left her family's cozy home in Boise, Idaho, embarking on what was supposed to be an exciting road trip to a small town outside Fresno, California. Her purpose? To meet with a renowned rabbit judge, a meeting that could potentially be a significant step in her aspiring career. The 27-year-old, always enthusiastic about new opportunities in her field, shared her plans with her boyfriend, Gerald Sanderson, and her parents, assuring them she would stay in touch. Gwen even mentioned the possibility of making a stop in Reno, Nevada, to break up the long drive.

However, as Gwen's journey progressed, an unsettling silence fell. Her usually active cellphone signal vanished, leaving both Gerald and her father, Andy, deeply concerned as their attempts to contact her went unanswered. Texts and calls echoed into a void, heightening the anxiety with each passing hour. By the next morning, the concern had escalated to alarm. Gerald, unable to shake the growing sense of dread, shared his fears with Gwen's parents. Recognizing the gravity of the situation, they promptly reported her missing to the Boise Police Department.

The mysterious circumstances surrounding Gwen's disappearance only deepened as investigators pieced together her movements from the moment she left her family home. What transpired in those critical hours is a perplexing tale, stitched together from surveillance footage and eyewitness accounts, painting a picture of Gwen's last known activities and her peculiar behavior.

Gwen's journey, which was expected to be straightforward, took an unusual turn just 20 miles from her Boise residence. In Nampa, a small town known for its quaint charm, Gwen made an unscheduled stop at a local convenience store. This seemingly mundane detail became crucial as it was the first in a series of puzzling actions. Both security footage and Gwen's debit card records confirmed her presence at the store, offering a tangible clue in the midst of uncertainty.

The surveillance footage from the store revealed more than just Gwen's presence; it unveiled a curious change in her appearance. When she left home, she was dressed casually in a blue shirt paired with Nike-brand tennis shoes, an outfit that spoke of comfort for a long drive. However, the Gwen captured by the store's cameras was markedly different. She had inexplicably changed into a red shirt and swapped her comfortable shoes for knee-high dress boots. This unexpected change in attire raised eyebrows and sparked questions. Moreover, the timing of her visit was peculiar. Gwen had embarked on her journey three hours earlier, yet had traveled only 20 miles, an unusually slow pace for such a short distance.

The next piece of the puzzle was found in surveillance footage dated June 27, 2023, at 12:00PM. Gwen was now in Jordan Valley, Oregon, a considerable distance from Nampa. At the Sinclair gas station, she was observed filling her car with gas. Following this, Gwen visited Mrs. Z's convenience store, a small establishment nestled in the valley. There, she purchased water and peanuts, mundane items that offered no clue to her state of mind. However, her inquiry about razors, an item out of place for her journey, added another layer of mystery. This odd request, coupled with her apparent hurry, as mentioned to the gas station attendant, painted a picture of a woman possibly grappling with more than just a road trip.

Yet, despite her claim of being in a hurry, Gwen was seen sitting in her car for an hour after her purchases. This unusual behavior caught the attention of the concerned gas station worker, who approached her to check if she was alright. Gwen reassured the worker that she was doing okay, but this interaction did little to ease the growing concerns about her well-being.

The days following Gwen's sudden and mysterious disappearance were fraught with tension and uncertainty. The small community of Jordan Valley, Malheur County, Oregon, became the unlikely epicenter of a baffling missing person case that captured the attention of both locals and the media. It was on June 30, 2023, three days after Gwen was officially reported missing, that a significant discovery was made – Gwen's car, a grey 2008 Honda Element, was found abandoned at Succor Creek, a serene and picturesque location in Malheur County, just a mile's deviation from the well-traveled Highway 95.

The car's presence in the area was not a recent occurrence. A UPS driver, going about his routine deliveries, had first noticed the Honda Element parked off the road during his lunch break on June 28th. However, it was only when a police officer, dispatched to the area for an unrelated matter, chanced upon the vehicle and ran its plates out of curiosity, that the connection to Gwen's missing person report came to light.

The discovery of the vehicle painted a perplexing picture. Positioned facing northeast, in an area frequented by visitors, the car was found unlocked, its key still dangling in the ignition, and the windows left partially open – as if abandoned in haste or left in a state of distraction. Inside the car, a scene of disarray and unanswered questions awaited. Gwen's leather shoulder bag lay there, containing her wallet, credit cards, and driver's license, alongside travel bags filled with personal items. The remnants of protein bar wrappers and empty soda cans were scattered about, hinting at a journey interrupted. Most heartbreakingly, three cages holding 11 rabbits were found inside, five of which had not survived. A water trough and a week's worth of food, thoughtfully prepared, lay unused.

In a curious twist, not far from the abandoned Honda Element, investigators stumbled upon Gwen's purple bathrobe, neatly folded as if used as a cushion, and the half-empty water jug she had purchased at a convenience store. These items, seemingly inconsequential, added layers of complexity to the already baffling case.

The discovery of Gwen's car spurred an extensive and desperate search. Investigators, alongside Gwen's family and friends, embarked on a comprehensive scouring of the area. They trudged on foot, maneuvered ATVs, and rode horseback across the rugged terrain, hoping to uncover any clue that might lead to Gwen. Four trained dogs were also employed, their keen senses a vital asset in the search efforts.

Despite the determined and exhaustive search, no significant breakthrough was made. The official search operation, having stretched the resources and resolve of the team, was reluctantly suspended on July 10, 2023, leaving more questions than answers.

The case, however, was far from closed. Two months later, on September 10, 2023, a new clue emerged, rekindling hope and curiosity. One of Gwen's t-shirts was found, snagged in a barbed wire fence about 1.5 miles from where her car had been discovered, near Dog Creek. This discovery, seemingly minor, prompted the search efforts to partially resume. Subsequently, her boots and a pair of mismatched socks were located approximately 80 yards south of the t-shirt. The boots, intriguingly, were placed in a crisscrossed manner, as if deliberately positioned.

The details of Gwen's appearance and the specifics of her vehicle were circulated widely. Gwendolyn Margaret "Gwen" Brunelle, 27 years old at the time of her disappearance, was last seen wearing a dark-colored t-shirt, black leggings, and distinctive black knee-high dress boots with a flat sole. Standing at 5'7" and weighing between 140-160 pounds, Gwen was recognizable by her brown eyes and long medium brown/auburn hair, usually tied up in a ponytail. Notable features included her pierced ears and the fact that she was left-handed. The grey 2008 Honda Element she drove bore Idaho license plates with the registration 5WT6X, a detail that had become a focal point in the ongoing investigation.

The pieces of the puzzle, fragmented and elusive, continued to perplex those involved in the case. Gwen's sudden disappearance, the condition in which her car was found, and the scattered personal items all formed a narrative riddled with mystery and speculation. The search for answers, fraught with dead ends and haunting questions, remained a deeply felt saga in the hearts of her family, friends, and a community touched by her unexplained vanishing.

Echo Lloyd

Echo Michelle Lloyd's life in Edwards, Missouri, unfolded like a serene landscape painting, with her nestled in a lake home, surrounded by a sprawling 10-acre canvas of nature. This rural setting, rich in wooded areas, resonated deeply with Echo, a 47-year-old mother of four adult children, who found unparalleled beauty in the natural world. Having transitioned to a quieter life, Echo reveled in the tranquility of her home, a welcome change after years bustling with the energy of raising Kelsey, Case, Caitlyn, and Kylie.

Just a year before, Echo's life had taken a significant turn. She moved to this picturesque property following a separation from her long-time husband, Tony. Born on May 23, 1972, in Pleasant Hill, Missouri, Echo grew up in a family deeply rooted in law enforcement. The friendships she forged in her childhood not only endured but also flourished into her adult years. Echo's journey into motherhood, culminating in the birth of her four children and later the joy of three grandchildren, was a fulfillment of her lifelong dream.

For years, Echo dedicated herself to being a stay-at-home mom, occasionally taking on various jobs, including caring for rescue dogs. Known for her caring and kindhearted nature, Echo was the epitome of a happy, outgoing spirit. Her love for helping others was only matched by her passion for the outdoors and her artistic flair.

However, Echo's sunny disposition belied the struggles she faced. In her

30s, as revealed in an interview on the Vanished podcast by her cousin, Echo endured a traumatic sexual assault by an acquaintance. This, coupled with past traumas, strained her marriage with Tony, leading to their eventual separation. The split was intended more as a breather than a permanent end, a chance for Echo to rediscover herself. Despite the distance, the family remained close-knit, and the bond with her children, especially Kelsey, remained unbreakable.

Echo cherished her independence at the lake house, pouring her heart into renovating it and making it truly her own. Her life there was a testament to her resilience and happiness. She maintained a strong relationship with Tony and held a special place in her daughter Kelsey's heart, who described her as the life of the party and her best friend.

On May 10, 2020, however, Echo's world shifted unexpectedly. It was Mother's Day, and Kelsey, bearing flowers and a card, arrived at her mother's home to find it unusually quiet. Echo's absence and unresponsive phone led Kelsey on a quest to locate her, reaching out to Echo's friends and returning to the house days later, only to find disturbing signs of her mother's sudden disappearance.

The plant Kelsey left on the porch had been moved, and the card was inside on Echo's dresser. After a fruitless search and no sign of Echo in the house or the neighboring areas, Kelsey's concern escalated into alarm. With Echo's car parked in the driveway but no trace of her inside, the silence in the house was deafening.

Kelsey Lloyd, grappling with the mysterious disappearance of her mother, Echo, was consumed by a growing sense of dread and urgency. As she waited for the Benton County Sheriff's Office to arrive at her mother's rural Missouri home, Kelsey's instincts told her something was terribly amiss. Her conviction that her mother was being held against her will only intensified as she frantically called out for Echo, her voice echoing through the surrounding woods.

The law enforcement's 30-minute journey to Echo's remote residence marked the beginning of an official investigation into her disappearance. Upon entering the house, Kelsey's concerns deepened. The once orderly home was in disarray, resembling a scene of a hasty ransack. Food, some of it moldy, lay scattered, and trash was piled up in corners. This chaos was uncharacteristic of Echo, who had always maintained a meticulous household, influenced by her obsessive-compulsive tendencies. Kelsey was adamant: this mess was not her mother's doing.

As investigators began piecing together the clues, they noted several items were missing, including Echo's car keys, cell phone, pistol, and prescription medication. Oddly, her purse, wallet, and ID were found discarded on the floor of her bedroom. Cigarettes, not of Echo's usual brand, and a lighter sat on her nightstand. The air conditioner was running at full blast, an unusual setting for Echo. Kelsey noted that the purse found at the scene was something Echo never left behind, not even for brief moments. The presence of her car, yet the absence of her keys, only deepened the mystery.

Despite these unsettling discoveries, the Sheriff's Office did not immediately classify the home as a crime scene. Extensive searches were conducted in the surrounding areas of Echo's 10-acre property, leading to the unexpected discovery of her missing pistol in a wooded area. However, further canine-assisted searches were abruptly called off, with authorities concluding Echo was likely not on the property.

The involvement of forensic scientists brought hope for new insights, but their findings remained undisclosed to both the family and the public. Kelsey, desperate for answers, reached out to Echo's cell phone provider and bank, only to learn there had been no activity since her disappearance. Echo's prescriptions, vital to her health, remained unfilled, casting doubt on the likelihood of her leaving voluntarily.

The Benton County Sheriff's Office, despite the accumulating anomalies, publicly stated there was no reason to suspect foul play. Sheriff Eric Knox expressed skepticism about Echo's ability to survive independently, given the lack of activity on her essential medications. Meanwhile, conflicting reports emerged about Echo's last known whereabouts, with multiple witnesses claiming to have seen her at different Dollar General stores. A receipt from a Walmart in Warsaw, dated on Mother's Day, suggested Echo had returned home that day, only to vanish without a trace.

As the investigation continued into June 2020, a month after Echo's disappearance, conflicting tips and the lack of concrete evidence left more questions than answers. The uncertainty surrounding Echo's fate, coupled with the absence of clear motives or suspects, painted a perplexing and haunting picture.

As the investigation progressed, Tony, Echo's ex-husband, inevitably fell under scrutiny, a common suspicion in such cases. Yet, those who knew the couple well attested to their amicable relationship post-separation. Tony's involvement in the search efforts and the children's recollections of a peaceful family life reinforced the belief in his innocence.

In a poignant interview with the Vanished podcast, Echo's children reminisced about a home where disagreements were rare and love was abundant, despite the eventual divergence in their parents' paths. Kelsey, Echo's stepdaughter, spoke of Tony's continued efforts to care for Echo while respecting her independence. Amidst the growing anxiety, a $7,000 reward was offered for information leading to Echo's whereabouts. The missing person's poster, detailing Echo's physical characteristics, her distinctive tattoos including the "Let It Be" inscription with birds, and the names of her children inked on her wrist, circulated widely, igniting a desperate search.

The Missouri State Highway Patrol's involvement some months later signified the complexity and seriousness of the case. Echo's family, especially her daughter Kelsey, remained adamant that Echo's disappearance was out of character. Echo, a rule-abiding, responsible individual, would never voluntarily sever contact, especially not with her newborn grandchild only a month old.

Kelsey and her family took it upon themselves to delve deeper, uncovering potential leads that seemed overlooked by the investigation. A notable incident at a Dollar General store in Warsaw, Missouri, where Echo reportedly appeared disoriented and mentioned her bank account being wiped out, raised alarms. The store clerk, familiar with Echo, noted her unusual behavior that day, yet this lead seemingly went unexplored by the authorities.

The family urged investigators to review surveillance footage from both Dollar General and Walmart, where a receipt dated on Mother's Day was found. This footage could potentially provide crucial insights into Echo's appearance and actions on the day she vanished. However, the availability and content of any such footage remained undisclosed to the public.

In June 2020, Kelsey established a Facebook page dedicated to finding her mother, using live streams to reach out to the community and share updates on the investigation. Her emotional resilience shone through, even as the strain of her mother's absence during significant family moments, like Thanksgiving, became increasingly evident.

By November 15, 2020, six months after Echo's disappearance, Kelsey's strength and determination were palpable. Her live updates not only kept the public engaged but also conveyed the depth of her love and commitment to finding her mother. The family's support of the Benton County Police Department and Sheriff Knox was unwavering, despite the slow progress and lack of concrete leads.

In a deeply personal reflection, Kelsey reminisced about the family gatherings that were now painfully incomplete without her mother. Echo, known for her leisurely pace in getting ready, had become a fond, humorous topic among her loved ones. They would often adjust event timings to accommodate Echo's routine, a quirk they dearly missed. Kelsey's candid sharing of these intimate family moments offered a glimpse into the vibrant life Echo led and the profound impact her disappearance had on those she loved.

Kelsey's pursuit for answers led her down a path filled with frustration and determination. Despite offering a staggering $99,000 reward for information and continuously advocating for her mother, the case remained shrouded in mystery. Kelsey's proactive approach saw her reaching out to various law enforcement agencies, seeking assistance beyond the local authorities. Her frustration was palpable as she encountered roadblocks and vague responses, especially from the Attorney General's office. The lack of progress and advice to remain quiet about the case only fueled her resolve to seek justice for her mother.

The family's suspicions soon turned towards a neighbor of Echo's, who had initially appeared friendly but gradually became a source of discomfort for Echo. This individual, who had unrestricted access to Echo's property and personal belongings, became increasingly intrusive and possessive, as recounted by Kelsey. Echo's discomfort with this neighbor's behavior, particularly his control over her finances and personal space, raised alarming concerns. Just weeks before her disappearance, Echo confided in Kelsey about the neighbor's overbearing presence, a revelation that later became a significant focal point in the investigation.

Despite Kelsey's insistence and the neighbor's suspicious behavior, including the peculiar incident with Echo's phone, law enforcement found no substantial evidence to implicate him. The neighbor's involvement in the search for Echo was sporadic and disinterested, further arousing suspicion among Echo's family and friends. This suspicion was compounded by a chilling discovery two weeks after Echo's disappearance: the neighbor's grandfather was found deceased in his basement.

Compounding the intrigue, prescription medications allegedly belonging to Echo were also reportedly found in the same basement. Despite these alarming discoveries, law enforcement did not obtain a search warrant for the neighbor's home, and the lack of an autopsy on the grandfather due to cremation left crucial questions unanswered.

Echo's family, determined to uncover the truth, delved into the background of the neighbor, identified as Josh. Conversations with Josh's ex-girlfriends revealed allegations of abusive behavior, painting a concerning picture of his character. Echo's cousin, in an interview on the Vanished podcast, brought forth claims of ATM footage showing Echo and Josh together, and a forensic audit of Echo's phone and financial records seemingly pointed to Josh's involvement. Josh's life underwent a drastic change after these events; he was removed from the house he shared with his grandfather and reportedly left the area.

The family's suspicions about Josh's manipulative abilities were further fueled by the belief that he might have influenced others to remain silent about any knowledge of Echo's fate. In July 2021, private investigator Jill, working independently, shared updates on the case. Her findings included statements from an informant who found Josh's grandfather and noted Josh's temperamental behavior, especially when drinking. Jill also relayed accounts of Josh's erratic actions in the weeks following Echo's disappearance, including a solitary camping trip and an incident where he abandoned his girlfriend and her child.

Amidst these revelations, Sheriff Knox of the Benton County Sheriff's Office reportedly identified a prime suspect, contradicting earlier statements about the lack of persons of interest. Jill's attempts to engage Josh in a conversation about the case yielded no results, adding to the mounting frustrations and mysteries.

As the second anniversary of Echo's disappearance approached, Kelsey continued to champion her mother's cause, despite the lack of new information from law enforcement. Her dedication led to the creation of a GoFundMe campaign to raise funds for posters, rewards, legal and search fees, and hiring a private investigator. Echo's cousin Mary echoed the family's sentiments, articulating the profound pain and unhealing wound caused by Echo's unexplained absence.

Kelsey's unwavering commitment to finding her mother was evident in her appeals for public support and involvement in the search efforts. She emphasized the need to keep Echo's story alive, highlighting her mother's wonderful personality and undeserved fate. In a significant update on June 10, 2023, Kelsey revealed that while investigators were no longer actively searching for Echo, the case remained open. This development, although disheartening, did not deter the family's resolve. The quest to uncover the truth about Echo Lloyd's disappearance continued, driven by a daughter's love and a community's support, in the hope of finally bringing closure to a case shrouded in mystery and heartache.

Paul Stevenson

As dawn broke on Sunday, March 11th, 2012, the sleepy city of Bundaberg in Queensland, Australia, was gently awoken by the first rays of the sun. It was just after 6:00 a.m., and the city, with its bustling centre and tranquil suburbs, began to stir. In one such suburb, a man named Paul Robert Stevenson was already embracing the day with a zest that was uniquely his. Dressed in his black leather jacket and jeans, Paul stepped out of his Sydney Street home, his motorcycle helmet under his arm, ready for an adventure.

Paul's love for his motorcycle was well-known. On this particular morning, he straddled his beloved bike and set off towards Mount Perry, a journey that would lead him in the direction of Paradise Dam. Little did anyone know, this ride would be unlike any other; Paul would never return.

Mount Perry, a small town nestled in the shadows of its namesake mountain, presents a stark contrast to the hustle and bustle of Bundaberg, known for its sugarcane fields and the famous Bundaberg Rum. The journey to Paradise Dam, located some 80 kilometres southwest of Bundaberg, promised a scenic ride along the Burnett River, leading to the serene Paradise Lake. This area, known for its breathtaking natural beauty, was a favorite among local motorcyclists like Paul, who cherished the freedom of the open road.

The route Paul chose was the Mount Perry-Jinjin Road, a popular country road winding through picturesque landscapes. While it offered stunning views, the road was also a busy thoroughfare, frequently traveled by locals and tourists alike. Paul's daughter, Nici Wellin, would later recount the sheer volume of traffic on this road, raising questions about how her father could have vanished without a trace on such a well-traveled path.

Paul's life was one deeply rooted in family and community. Married to his wife Julie since 1990, the couple had two children, Nicky and Tom. Paul was the epitome of a dedicated father, deeply involved in his children's lives, whether it was presiding over the local junior Football Club or hosting barbecues in their backyard. An article from Nicky in "That's Life" magazine painted a vivid picture of their happy, close-knit family life.

Professionally, Paul was a diesel fitter, a skilled mechanic specializing in diesel engines. His work was demanding, but Paul's expertise and dedication provided well for his family. Outside of work, his passions included a project that was uniquely his own – restoring a classic 1978 Honda CB750. This motorcycle, a revered model in biking circles, was a fixer-upper when Paul acquired it. Through diligent work and a keen mechanical mind, Paul brought the bike back to its former glory, much to his and his family's delight.

Paul's rides were not just for leisure; he often participated in charity runs to support local cancer research. These rides, sometimes solo and other times accompanied by his son Tom, reflected Paul's generous spirit and his desire to give back to the community.

Described by those who knew him as intelligent, outgoing, and exceedingly funny, Paul was a man who loved life and those around him. He was a pillar in his community, always ready to lend a hand or share a laugh. But above all, Paul was a family man, always there for his loved ones in times of joy and challenge.

The day before his disappearance, Paul's family celebrated a significant milestone – his and Julie's 22nd wedding anniversary. It was a joyous occasion, made even more special by the announcement of Nicky's pregnancy. Paul's reaction to the news, filled with excitement and love, epitomized the kind of father and person he was.

Paul Stevenson was not just an experienced rider; he was a connoisseur of the road, a man who found joy not in the speed but in the journey itself. Each curve and each scenic backdrop was a part of his meditation, his escape into the serene landscapes that surrounded Bundaberg. On that Sunday morning, Paul's plan was simple yet filled with the small joys of life. After his ride, he intended to return home for a refreshing shower before heading to the Football Club, where he served as president, for a 9:00 a.m. meeting. The day was to be capped off with a leisurely afternoon visiting friends with his family. But fate had other plans, and Paul's routine journey turned into a perplexing mystery.

Paul's daughter, Nicky, cherished the last moments she shared with her father. Their bond was evident in the simple yet profound gestures of a farewell kiss and a loving goodbye. Known to struggle with insomnia, it was commonplace for Paul to be up before dawn, often finding solace in early morning rides. The ride on Sunday, March 11th, seemed no different. He was a silhouette against the twilight, riding into the morning light, unbeknownst to his family that it would be the last time they'd see him.

As the hours ticked by, a sense of unease began to settle over the Stevenson household. Paul's absence grew more conspicuous with each passing moment. Both Julie, his wife, and Nicky started to frantically reach out to him via calls and texts, but all attempts met with silence. This was uncharacteristic of Paul, who was always punctual and communicative. The unanswered calls and texts were out of the ordinary, raising alarm bells in their minds.

By the time the clock struck 6 p.m., and Paul's phone went straight to voicemail, the worry turned into outright panic. Julie's call to the football club brought a chilling revelation; Paul had not been seen there all day. The pieces of the puzzle were not fitting together, and the Stevenson family was left grappling with a barrage of worrisome thoughts. Had Paul encountered an accident? Was he lying in a hospital somewhere, or worse?

Nicky and her boyfriend Brenton took to the streets, tracing the route they believed Paul might have taken towards the dam. They scoured every inch of the road, eyes peeled for any sign of Paul or his motorcycle, but their search was in vain. The night was restless, filled with anxiety and unanswerable questions about Paul's whereabouts and well-being.

As dawn broke on Monday, March 12th, with no sign of Paul, the family's concern escalated into action. They arrived at the police station early, eager to get the help they desperately needed. The police took their concerns seriously, recognizing the unlikelihood of Paul having disappeared voluntarily. The ensuing search was a massive undertaking. More than 200 individuals, including police, volunteers, family, friends, and even indigenous trackers, combed the area, supplemented by the efforts of tracking dogs and helicopters.

Bundaberg police inspector Kev Gutteridge expressed his astonishment at the lack of clues, echoing the sentiments of the search party. The extent of the search was unprecedented, covering vast areas and leaving no stone unturned. Yet, Paul seemed to have vanished without a trace. Nicky, reflecting on the immense efforts, was baffled by the absence of any leads.

The unfolding mystery of Paul Stevenson's disappearance took a turn towards the enigmatic when a psychic claimed to have a vision of him. In this vision, they saw Paul near a steep embankment, suggesting he may have fallen. This claim coincided with a distressing dream that Nicky, Paul's daughter, had about the mountain ranges of Mount Perry. Desperate for any lead, she relayed both the psychic's vision and her dream to the authorities.

The search for Paul intensified, with police visiting local businesses in search of surveillance footage that might shed light on his whereabouts. Their persistence paid off when they uncovered footage from the early morning of Paul's disappearance. At around 3:28 a.m., Paul was captured on camera stopping to refuel his motorcycle. This was the last known sighting of him that morning. For a man known to be an early riser due to insomnia, being out at this hour was unusual, even by his standards.

The second day of the search brought a glimmer of hope. A rescue helicopter, piloted by Dick Snell, flew over the area between Gin Gin and Mount Perry. Around 10:45 a.m., something caught their eye near a bend in the road. Lowering for a closer look, they spotted a motorcycle lying on its side, partially hidden by foliage, with a black helmet beside it. The location was immediately radioed down to investigators, who rushed to the scene near the Wamba winery along Gin Gin–Mount Perry Road. There, they found Paul's prized 1978 Honda motorcycle.

Nicky's phone rang with the news from the Bundaberg police – Paul's bike had been found, but Paul was nowhere to be seen. Under the bike, a few snakes had taken shelter, suggesting the bike had been there for some time. The bike and helmet were found down the embankment, with some damage to the bike but nothing indicating a major collision. Strangely, Paul's helmet and saddlebags appeared to have been hidden near the bike, raising more questions than answers.

The scene was puzzling. While the bike and helmet were recovered, other personal items such as Paul's wallet, keys, phone, sunglasses, and binoculars were missing. There had been no activity on his key card or cell phone since his disappearance. The absence of skid marks or blood at the scene suggested that if there had been an accident, it hadn't been severe.

Theories abounded. Some speculated that Paul might have taken a hike and gotten lost, given his love for the outdoors and the missing binoculars. Others wondered if he might have sustained a hand injury, become confused, and wandered off. Yet, there was no concrete evidence to support any of these theories.

The search operation, massive in scale, was officially called off after four days, although friends and family continued their own efforts. Despite the extensive search, Paul remained missing, and no further clues as to his whereabouts emerged.

In a public plea, both authorities and the family urged anyone with information to come forward. Considering the busy road and the time of Paul's ride, it was hard to believe that no one had seen anything. The discovery of the bike had brought hope, but it quickly turned to despair as Paul's whereabouts remained a mystery.

Police attempted to trace Paul's phone but were unsuccessful, likely due to poor cell reception in the area. Inspector Gutteridge, speaking to The Courier Mail, remarked on the uniqueness of the case, comparing it to the mysterious disappearance of Queensland Police officer Mick Isles in 2009.

In an innovative attempt to gather information, authorities placed a mannequin at the spot where Paul's bike was found, holding a sign asking for information. This led to a potential breakthrough when witnesses reported seeing a man matching Paul's description walking along the road on the day of his disappearance, not far from where the bike was found.

In the aftermath of Paul Stevenson's mysterious disappearance, his family grappled with a myriad of emotions and theories, but one thing was clear: they could not fathom the idea that Paul had simply wandered off or gotten lost. The possibility of foul play loomed large in their minds, a theory that seemed more plausible than any accidental or voluntary departure. Nicky Stevenson, at the forefront of the quest for answers, was adamant in her belief that someone, somewhere, held the key to the puzzle of her father's fate. Her conviction was unwavering, fueled by the baffling nature of his vanishing in a world where disappearing without a trace seemed almost impossible.

A year after Paul's disappearance, the family orchestrated a unique event known as "Green Day" to mark the somber anniversary. The color green, symbolizing hope, was chosen to unite the community in solidarity with the Stevenson family and others who had lost loved ones without a trace. The initiative, covered in a feature by the Western Star, aimed to draw broader attention to Paul's case and the plight of all missing persons. Residents were encouraged to wear green, a visual testament to the collective yearning for answers and closure.

As time marched on, the Stevenson family oscillated between theories of foul play and other, less tangible possibilities. The case remained as baffling to investigators as it was on day one. Despite an open and active investigation, leads were virtually non-existent. All that was ever found were Paul's motorcycle and helmet, leaving a trail that went cold almost as soon as it was discovered.

In a poignant twist of fate, Nicky's first daughter, Mia, was born three months after Paul's disappearance. Mia grew up hearing stories about the grandfather she never met, and in her innocent childhood manner, she would look up at the stars and blow kisses to the grandfather she knew only through tales and photographs.

Four years after Paul vanished, a coroner's inquest was convened. With no new evidence or sightings, Paul was officially declared deceased. The family organized a memorial, not as a definitive goodbye but as a celebration of his life. The memorial was a testament to the man Paul was – a beloved figure in his community, a dedicated family man, and a motorcycle enthusiast who found joy in the simple pleasure of a ride.

Paul Stevenson, at the time of his disappearance, was described as a white male with brown hair and eyes, standing approximately 178 centimeters tall. He was last seen on surveillance footage refueling his black 1978 Honda motorcycle, which was later found down an embankment, 16 kilometers east of Mount

Perry Township. Despite extensive searches and investigations, Paul has never been found, and the only potential sighting remains unconfirmed.

As the years passed, theories about Paul's fate continued to circulate. Some believed he might have been a victim of foul play, while others thought he might have ventured into the wilderness and succumbed to an accident or natural causes. Yet another theory, though less favored by the family and authorities, suggested that Paul might have intentionally disappeared. However, this theory seemed unlikely given Paul's apparent contentment with his life and his close ties to his family.

The Stevenson family's life changed dramatically in the wake of Paul's disappearance. Once joyous occasions like Christmas became subdued and tinged with sadness. Their contact with authorities dwindled over time, with no new developments to report. They were left to mourn at the spot where his bike was found, the only tangible link to Paul's last known moments.

Nicky's reflections in an interview with The Courier Mail captured the enduring heartache and disbelief. The family continued to hope for his return, finding it hard to accept the reality of his absence. Paul Stevenson was more than just a missing person; he was a pillar of his family, a contributor to his community, and a man who embraced life with open arms. His disappearance left a void that extended far beyond the confines of his immediate family, affecting everyone who knew him.

As the years passed, the mystery surrounding Paul Stevenson's disappearance remained as deep and impenetrable as ever. Theories abounded, but without concrete evidence, they remained just that – theories. In a case shrouded in uncertainty, with scant clues and no definitive answers, the family and community were left to grapple with the haunting question: what really happened to Paul Stevenson?